LABOUR'S WRONGS AND LABOUR'S REMEDY

LABOUR'S WRONGS

AND LABOUR'S REMEDY

OR

THE AGE OF MIGHT

AND THE AGE OF RIGHT

BY

JOHN F. BRAY

[1839]

REPRINTS OF ECONOMIC CLASSICS

Augustus M. Kelley · Publishers
NEW YORK 1968

1975

First Edition 1839

LEEDS: PUBLISHED BY DAVID GREEN, BRIGGATE

J. GUEST, STEEL HOUSE-LANE, BIRMINGHAM
A. HEYWOOD, OLDHAM-STREET, MANCHESTER
AND SOLD BY ALL BOOKSELLERS

Reprinted 1968 by

AUGUSTUS M. KELLEY · PUBLISHERS

New York   New York   10010

Library of Congress Catalogue Card Number

67-19708

PRINTED IN THE UNITED STATES OF AMERICA
by SENTRY PRESS, NEW YORK, N. Y. 10019

LABOUR'S WRONGS

AND LABOUR'S REMEDY;

OR,

THE AGE OF MIGHT

AND THE AGE OF RIGHT.

BY J. F. BRAY.

"We are a numerous people, and we want strength! We have an excellent soil, and we are destitute of provision! We are active and laborious, and we live in indigence! We pay enormous tributes, and we are told that they are not sufficient! We are at peace without, and our persons and property are not safe within! What, then, is the secret enemy that devours us?"—*Ruins of Empires.*

LEEDS:

PUBLISHED BY DAVID GREEN, BRIGGATE;

J. GUEST, STEELHOUSE-LANE, BIRMINGHAM
A. HEYWOOD, 60, OLDHAM-STREET, MANCHESTER;
AND SOLD BY ALL BOOKSELLERS.

1839.

PREFACE.

Whenever any crisis in the affairs of men is about to take place, there is ever to be found a number of people ready to preach up things as they are. These champions fight stoutly and cunningly against the innovation of existing institutions and modes of acting; and they endeavour to reason the sensible and alarm the timid into remaining quiet, and enduring meekly whatever evils they may be afflicted with. Belonging to one class, and having in view a common object, these alarmists attempt to convince the people that everything is almost as well as it can be—that few evils are endured by them which are not necessary consequences of existence—that their governmental burthens may be alleviated by gradual and imperceptible reforms—that the present gradations of society, which cause so much discontentment among the poor and the oppressed, have always existed, and therefore ever must exist—and that any attempts of the productive classes to better themselves by interfering with this "natural arrangement of society," will be attended with the most disastrous results to themselves.

Notwithstanding the sage advice and the gloomy fore-bodings of these friends of the people, the latter are perpetually endeavouring to the utmost of their power, by means of political and trades' unions, to alter the present state of things, and keep to themselves that vast amount of wealth which is annually taken from them by existing usages. But, conscious of having justice on their side, the productive classes have hitherto regarded the end more than the means; and the first has been unattainable only because the latter were inadequate. The equality of social and political rights which the masses have so long contended for, is consonant with reason and justice, or it is not. If it be not, then should their ignorance and injustice be exposed by those whose rights and privileges the people are trespassing upon by their assumption of equality. But if such equality of rights be in accordance with the immutable principles of truth and justice, then are the people bound to contend for it wholly and immediately; and to cease praying, piecemeal, for that which ought to be conceded to them unhesitatingly, and at once.

The diversity of opinion which exists on political matters, and the anomalies seen in connection with a merely political equality, call for more evidence than has yet been given of the peculiar efficacy of any particular governmental remedy to accomplish the end desired. To acquire such evidence by reasoning from first principles, and by a rigid comparison of theory with fact, should be the first great object of the productive classes, and the prelude to all demands for change. Had they not been thus deficient in the knowledge of principles, they would not now have had to mourn over the fate of the many powerful political and trades' combinations which have been wrecked in the vain endeavours to obtain redress for their wrongs. Unless men discover and remove causes, they can never escape from consequences. Whatever may be the conclusions arrived at by such an examination, in regard to the excellence of particular governmental reforms, or the fitness or unfitness of the present social system, the inquiry cannot but serve the cause of truth. Ignorance itself, in its blind gropings for the unknown and undefined, often accidentally stumbles upon truths which years of laborious and systematic application have failed to bring to light.

From their present condition and future prospects, there is no class of the community which political or social changes can concern more nearly than they do the productive classes; and none are more imperatively called upon to search for the truth, and look into the future. Hanging, as the economists say they are, " on the skirts of existence,"—living, as so many thousands of them do, from hand to mouth—the producers are at the mercy, and bear almost the entire brunt, of every storm which interferes with or disturbs the existing arrangements of society, political or commercial. No unfavourable circumstance acts upon one class, which does not instantly re-act with double force upon the productive class—no loss is suffered by any portion of the community, which the latter class have not eventually to make good. Thus situated—thus placed, by their position, at the mercy of men and classes who can have no fellow-feeling with them—it behoves the producers to determine whether their present condition may not be improved, and to discover what are the particular means whereby such improvement may be effected. The experience of every year and every day teaches them, that, however circumscribed may be their knowledge of the causes which have led to the existing state of things, they cannot know less than those who have hitherto professed to govern and direct them. The time for blind submisson to established authorities and usages is passing away ; for no important event transpires which does not proclaim the utter inability of rulers in general to conceive of, and their complete incapacity to cope with or direct, the great truths and principles which are every day coming into view.

If the productive classes would be successful in their search for a remedy, they must proceed in the path of discovery unfettered by those notions which are so sedulously instilled into them, respecting their own inferiority

and the eternity of existing usages. As men, and apart
from their present position as a poor governed class,
oppressed by a rich governing class, the producers have
nothing to do with the alleged sacredness of established institutions: they have merely to determine whether it be not possible to change *that social whole which
keeps them poor*, as well as that governmental part which
oppresses them because they are poor. The requisite
knowledge can be obtained only by going at once to first
principles. In the words of one who has made many
efforts to uphold the present system, we are now in " the
very condition, if the people could but see it, for the
exercise of faith in principles. With a dark and shifting
near future, and a bright and fixed ultimate destiny, what
is the true, the only wisdom? Not to pry into the fogs
or thickets round about, or to stand still for fear of what
may next occur in the path; but to look from Eden gate
behind to heaven gate before, and press on to the certain
future. In his political as in his moral life, man should,
in the depth of his ignorance and the fallibility of his
judgment, THROW HIMSELF, IN THE FULL SENSE OF
SECURITY, UPON PRINCIPLES; and then he is safe from
being depressed by opposition, or scared by uncertainty, or
depraved by responsibility."

INTRODUCTION.

If it were ever possible to predict what shall be, from a consideration of what has been—if ever the signs of the times gave warning of great troubles or changes—there is that in the present which tells us, in a manner not to be misunderstood, that the hour for the final conflict between Right and Might cannot be far distant. That it is time the event took place, let the wrongs of man for forty cen turies testify—that it is time to put an end to the bondage of labour, let the sufferings of the millions of her martyred children bear witness !

From the nature of things there must be a cause for every effect, however concealed or inscrutable that cause may be ; and of all causes, none are of so much importance as those from which emanate the wide-spread poverty and discontentment which exist at the present time through-out the whole world—and, more especially, in those nations calling themselves civilised. The numerous remedies proposed, tried, and rejected, one after the other, do not prove that it is impossible to change, for the better, this unnatural state of things ; such ill success merely shews that the world at large—nations as well as governments—are as yet ignorant of the origin and the nature of the great wrong which has preyed upon man for so many ages.

Of all nations on the face of the earth, the people of the United Kingdom suffer the most severely, and are, there-fore, the most in want of a remedy. Throughout the country, distrust or dissatisfaction is universal. Not one class of society is at rest ; but a troubled and uneasy sensation—a kind of forerunner of evil or of change—per-

vades alike the bosoms of both the rich and the poor—
the tramplers and the trampled upon.

Whatever may be the condition in which society now
is, it could not, from the very nature of its component
parts, and the circumstances which have for ages operated
upon and influenced those parts, be different from what it
is; and however alarming the present state of things
may appear to the unjust man and the extortioner, there
is in the prospect nothing that can terrify the honest and
the industrious, wherever they may be.

The productive classes are bewildered amidst the multiplicity of remedies offered for their consideration. They
have as many remedies as wrongs—one contradicting
another, and most of them equally valueless; for they are
alike based merely on passing events, instead of resting on
the broad foundation of some great principle. That
which appears to be a remedy in one year, turns out, in
the next year, to be no remedy whatever; for the particular evil which such remedy applied to, is found to have
shifted its locality, or changed to some secondary evil.

There is wanted, not a mere governmental or particular
remedy, but a general remedy—one which will apply to
all social wrongs and evils, great and small. The productive classes want a remedy for their incessant toil—they
want a remedy for their compulsory idleness—they want
a remedy for their poverty—they want a remedy for the
misery, and ignorance, and vice, which such toil, such
idleness, and such poverty produce.

Although it may appear difficult to obtain such a
remedy, it will be seen, hereafter, that it is anything but
impossible. All sciences are more or less imperfect; but
of all sciences, politics, or the science of human government, is the least understood, although its great book has
been open to the inspection of man for four thousand
years. Man has made so little progress, because it is in the
nature of good or bad forms of government, and institutions, and states of society, to perpetuate themselves, and
keep successive generations in one continuous mode of
thinking and of acting. Men, in general, go not to the
first principles of things; they take the world as they find
it, and look only to the state of society, the form of
government, or the religion of their country, for the time
being. But the nonage of intellect is passing away, and

the mind of man will soon take a wider and a bolder flight than any it has yet dared to contemplate. Had the land-marks of Europe always been kept in sight, America would still have been unknown to us; and, unless we boldly overleap the boundaries which custom and prece-dent has placed around us—bou⸱ iaries which shut man out from all but the lower and ɔaser portions of intel-lectual and physical existence—we shall never behold nor possess that vast and beautiful region of human felicity, which, from the nature of things, cannot but have existence.

All other sciences are but as steps to the science of government. They all add something to man's knowledge of himself, his capabilities, and his true position in refer-ence to external objects. What is it that the mind of man, if properly directed, cannot accomplish? What other finite being has attributes so mighty—and yet, what other thing existing is so helpless and so wretched? We can roam through the universe with the astronomer, and look on solar systems, and behold planets and their satel-lites rolling in ponderous majesty through the illimitable ocean of space: we can, with the geologist, go back to times when history was not—when our earth, occupying a different position in space, and peopled by widely differ-ent modifications of being to any now existing, knew not man, nor his crimes, nor his follies: we can progress, with the historian, from as far back as human records extend, up to the present time, and survey man under the innu-merable systems of religion and forms of government which have cursed him from his creation—making the earth one vast slaughter-yard, and defiling it with execrable pollution: we can, with the chemist, dissolve the chains which bind together the elements of existing forms of matter, and, from their wreck, produce a new creation, and bestow on things new properties and appear-ances: we can, with the anatomist and the metaphysician, study the nature of our own corporeal and mental being, and observe the inseparable dependency of mind on matter, and the influence of external circumstances upon both: we can view every variety of human action, and can discover the various incentives to such action: we can, as it were, live over again the times that are past—ourselves commit-ting the crime, and judging the offender, and meting out the award. And thus, having the accumulated knowledge and experience of all past ages to guide him, and the accumulated errors and miseries of all past ages to warn him—imbued with the spirit, as well as acquainted with the letter, of history—what is man not prepared to achieve ?

The untiring mind of man is ever in search of what it has never yet found—happiness; but because this ultimate end of all human exertion has not hitherto been attained, it does not follow that man should give up his search, and die. His physical organization is as perfect as that of any other being with which he is acquainted, while his mental powers far exceed those of any other known intelligence. It would, then, be an unseemly gap in the harmonious adaptation and continuous perfection which runs through all creation, if the powers and attributes possessed by man could do nothing towards removing that misery and dissatisfaction which has for so many ages been the portion of his race. To assert that, amidst a universe of joy, man alone is born to sorrow and to trouble, is to commit a foul libel upon the Almighty and perfect disposer of all things !

Were man a stationary being, like the beasts and birds by which he is surrounded—had he a fixed and unchangeable instinct, instead of a progressive and improvable reason—any change in his social institutions would be unnecessary. Society would have been the same at the beginning as it is at present ; and it would continue in one uniform state as long as man should exist. But man is not thus stationary ; he is a reasoning, and therefore a progressing, being. The knowledge and experience of one generation can be transmitted to the next ; and, as a man at forty years of age must possess more knowledge than he did at twenty, so also must the world at large possess a greater accumulation of knowledge at the end of four thousand years from the creation of man, than was possessed at the end of four hundred. Knowledge is merely an accumulation of facts ; and wisdom is the art of applying such knowledge to its true purpose—the promotion of human happiness. Although men may have much knowledge, and no wisdom, there can only be little wisdom where there is but little knowledge. The present generation have the accumulated knowledge and experience of four thousand years to work upon ; and therefore they have it in their power to act wiser, in respect to the establishment of social and political institutions, than any generation that has preceded them.

Such being the nature of man, and such his powers, the consideration of a social change need excite no more surprise or apprehension than a simple political movement. If a social change be a gigantic one, so, likewise, are the evils mighty which require to be removed. Throughout the whole universe, from the most stupendous planet to the individual atom, changes are perpetual—there is nothing at rest—nothing stationary; to affirm, therefore, that governmental institutions require no reformation—that social systems need no alteration—is just as absurd as to say that the man shall wear the swaddling clothes which befitted his infancy ; and be pleased, in maturity, with the rattle which charmed his childhood.

States of society and forms of government have always been forced upon men by the common march of events ; and that state of society or form of government which existed at one period of a nation's history, and was sufficient for all its wants, will never be tolerated at a later period. Who, at the present day, would wish to return to a state of society, with its accompanying manners, and form of government, and religious institutions, such as existed in Great Britain in the time of the Druids, or the Romans, or the Saxons, or the Normans ? How many Protestants would wish to revive the days when Catholicism was in its glory and its power, and the brand of persecution dried up the blood of the martyrs ? All these changes were but manifestations of the common progress of things ; and they all happened naturally and unavoidably, independent of the control of governments or individuals. Catholicism succeeded Paganism, then Protestantism came after Catholicism, and both are now being superseded by Dissent ; and all the evils which these changes brought upon the people of other days, as well as all the miseries that have befallen nations in our own times, are solely attributable to the insane and blasphemous endeavours of human rulers to set up their authority against the fiat of the Almighty, and tell man he shall go no further. And have all the treasures wasted, and the blood spilled—all the persecutions, and punishments

and revolting crimes which have taken place to keep man
and his institutions stationary, effected the object for
which they were intended? Turn to history for an
answer—look back from our days to the days of our fore-
fathers, and ask if any of the many powerful endeavours to
prevent changes ever yet succeeded.

At no period since the creation of the world has man
been so well prepared, as he is at present, to effect a
change in the very constitution of society; and no other
nation possesses so many facilities for commencing such a
change, and carrying it forward successfully, as do the
people of the United Kingdom. A variety of circumstances, which have not had so much influence on other
countries, have tended to induce this ripeness in ourselves.
We suffer greater burthens than any other people on earth
—burthens which our unceasing industry only just enables
us to bear up against, and live. We have a greater
amount of fixed capital, or accumulated labour, in the
form of roads, railways, canals, manufactories, and machinery of every description, than is possessed by any
other nation. We are collected together in large masses, and
have excellent means of communication. As a people, we
have as much political knowledge, and as much incipient
union among ourselves, as any other nation. The entire
mass of the producers, with a great portion of the distributors of wealth, are groaning under the accumulated
wrongs of centuries of misgovernment and mismanagement.
They have tried almost every conceivable means to obtain
relief and redress, but they have ever been betrayed, and
disappointed, and cheated with a shadow. Men have at
length, however, begun to look from the tyrant to the
tyranny—from the effect to the cause. Thus our present
position augurs well for a social change, and for the advancement of man's highest destiny.

It is only when men suffer great wrongs, that they look
about for great remedies. So long as they are satisfied
with their worldly condition, whether it be good or bad,
they will not think of changes: they will not give up a
certain moderate good for an uncertain great benefit.
While the people of the United Kingdom were thus comparatively contented with their means of enjoyment, they
thought neither of states of society, nor forms of government, nor the rights of man: as the present social system

produced its natural effects—as toil grew more and pay grew less—men began to think upon the matter, and to devise remedies: but now, when the condition of the productive classes is so bad that no change can make it worse, they are ready to adopt almost any remedy which promises relief.

We have at length arrived at the exact time when a mighty change can take place with the greatest benefit to the mass, and the least injury to individuals. The people are so much enlightened as to be capable of proceeding to remedy their disorders calmly and dispassionately ; and, as yet, they are not so maddened by long suffering and hopelessness of relief, as to rush blindly upon the unfortunate authors of their wrongs, and hurl down all in indiscriminate destruction. At an earlier period we were unripe for a great social change; and, if we permit existing evils to go on unredressed, an ultimate movement will be not the less certain, while, instead of being conducted in peace and order, it will be fearfully convulsive, and will bury alike, in one common grave, the good and the bad—the patriot and the despot.

On the broad principle of equal rights will Labour now take its stand,—not Labour in the United Kingdom only, but in France, and the United States, and the world at large. This principle will apply equally to men of all countries, all colours, and all creeds. We will survey undisguised and uncovered, that Great Enemy which has devoured the people of all nations, in all times ; and we shall find out the manner, and the only manner, in which the power of this enemy may be subdued and annihilated. Let Labour, then, come to the battle fearlessly.

CHAPTER I.

THE WRONGS OF MAN, AND THEIR ORIGIN.

" We are a numerous people, and we want strength ! We have an excellent soil, and we are desitute of provision ! We are active and laborious, and we live in indigence ! We pay enormous tributes, and we are told that they are not sufficient ! We are at peace without, and our persons and property are not safe within ! What, then, is the secret enemy that devours us ?"

THUS have asked, for ages, the toil-worn and the oppressed people of all so-called civilised countries. Numerous have been the answers given to this question; but we, as one people who have made the inquiry, are still overworked and indigent—still burthened with enormous taxation—still the slaves and the prey of a secret enemy ; a remedy for this state of things, therefore, has not been discovered, or, if discovered, we have by some means been prevented from making use of it. Before we can determine whether such a remedy has yet offered itself, it will be necessary not only that we should be acquainted with our wrongs, but likewise with the nature and origin of those wrongs. Unless we thus go to the cause of the evil, we shall never do more than remove one wrong to make way for another.

The whole history of man, from his creation to the present day, is but one long record of crime, and bloodshed, and suffering. Man has always been wronged by his fellow-man, and has always been in search of remedies ; but, no matter where he has lived, or what religion he has professed, or what form of government he has established, the result of his search has always been the same—the means employed have ever failed to accomplish the end desired. All history tolls the same funereal knell to human hopes and human happiness.

Amongst the many political and theological institutions which have at times been established, not one form of government or system of religion can be found, which has not been subject to frequent alteration and revision. There have always been revolutions, or occasions for them. But these changes and revolutions have never yet touched the social system; they have only alleviated or modified the minor wrongs which the system itself brought into existence. Man has been operated upon by almost every variety of circumstance which this system can give rise to; he has been at one time an ignorant and ungoverned savage—at another, a citizen of a republic of civilised and highly polished barbarians—and, again, the trembling slave of a despot : he has been without religion, and with religion, and by turns all religions—yet still, though all this time and all these changes, man has been the same restless and dissatisfied being—he has been any thing and every thing but THE MAN which the faculties given by the Creator will render him capable of becoming. The masses of all nations have been alike poor, and persecuted, and miserable, under republics as well as monarchies—under every known modification of government by the few and government by the many—which cannot but lead men to suspect that a mere form of government is not the secret enemy which devours them; and that, therefore, no governmental change can destroy this enemy.

But there are those who deny that we have any wrongs to be removed, or that the productive classes suffer any ills which are not necessary consequences of existence, and which are therefore irremediable. Where is the man whose honest hands toil for his daily bread, that is unconscious that he bears with wrongs and injuries which ought to be, and which may be, removed? Are not such engraved upon the hearts and minds of men as with a pen of iron? What are the working classes of every nation but beasts of burthen, without hearts and without souls, whose doom it is to labour and to die ! Has not every epithet of scorn and hate which brainless pride could call to mind, been heaped upon them ? What is the garb of labour but a sign of ignorance, or infamy, or political nonentity ? If taxes are to be levied, the workers must pay them—if a war be undertaken, they must go out to fight—if unjust laws be enacted, they must obey without murmuring—if they complain of tyranny, and dare to resist, they are slaughtered like wild beasts! The very marrow of their bones, and the life-blood of their children, is drunk up with excessive toil!

How comes it to pass, that those who are the very life and soul of this great nation, are thus trampled upon, and despised, and defied? They have heads to think, and hearts to feel, and hands to execute—they form, conjointly, a mighty mass—their capability of doing either good or evil is bounded only by their will. With such gigantic powers, how is it that they are thus weak? The reasons are these: they are weak because they are disunited—they are disunited because there is a diversity of opinion as to what is the enemy which devours them—they are ignorant of a remedy for their wrongs because they have not themselves sought for one. They have ever looked for relief where it could not possibly be found. They have sought for council and assistance from classes and castes who had a direct though mistaken interest in misleading, dividing, and oppressing them. They have idly chimed in with the opinion of this or that non-producer, or the opposite opinion of this or that member of parliament, or the again differing opinion promulgated in this or that newspaper; and they have thus been led to hope for benefit from measures which, as they have no connection with the cause of their wrongs, are necessarily powerless and worthless. They must be no longer thus led like children; but proceed at once, with cool heads and determined hearts, to obtain that political and social salvation which can be theirs only through their own exertions.

What, then, is the secret enemy which devours us? It stands before us as a mighty tree, whose wide-spread roots, deep seated in the soil of Labour, draw up the dew of life and health, and leave the parent and the creator powerless and impoverished. We would remove this enemy; and what are the means recommended and adopted for the purpose? Are we endeavouring to destroy its barrenising influence for ever, by tearing it up? No; some advisers cry out—"Cut off this root"—others, "Cut off that"; some tell us to tear away a branch which is high up, and others, again, point to another branch lower down. The productive class thus become lost amidst the conflicting opinions they daily meet with, and are ever seeking, never finding. The narrow views and baneful prejudices which a contracted system of education has compelled us to adopt, have almost rendered us incapable of seeing or comprehending Labour's enemy *as a whole*, although each of us feels the blighting influence or sees the deformity of some particular part; for our enemy, like the triple god of the Hindoo, shews us a different face from every side on which we view it. The only way to arrive at truth is to go at once to First Principles. Instead, then, of confining our inquiries to the benefits and the evils resulting from particular forms of government, and regarding monarchies and aristocracies alone as the Great Enemy, and the prime originators of wrong,—let us take a wider range, and go at once to the source from whence governments themselves have arisen; and we shall soon discover that all of them are but as boughs of the great tree of human evil—that they are only as the claws with which the Great Enemy seizes upon Labour's substance—and that, although we may distinguish them by the names of monarchies and republics, yet the attributes of each are the same, the ends of each are the same, the wrongs inflicted upon the working classes by each are the same. By thus going to the origin of the thing, we shall find that every form of government, and every social and governmental wrong, owes its rise to the existing social system—*to the institution of property as it at present exists*—and that, therefore, if we would end our wrongs and our miseries at once and for ever, THE PRESENT ARRANGEMENTS OF SOCIETY MUST BE TOTALLY SUBVERTED, and supplanted by those more in accordance with the principles of justice and the rationality of man.

" Equal rights and equal laws," has long been the war-cry of the working classes of Great Britain; and they have all hoped and expected to obtain this one thing needful by mere governmental changes. What is meant by Equal Rights and Equal Laws ? The words themselves plainly express their own meaning; and yet there is scarcely a sentence to be found which has been interpreted so many different ways, and made to signify such a variety of meanings. Some men, when they speak of equal rights, mean thereby simply that there should be universal suffrage, vote by ballot, and free admission to Parliament; while others, again, advancing rather nearer to first principles, call for the complete subversion of the monarchy, and the establishment of a republic. By some of these professed advocates of justice, the political institutions of the United States are held up to us as models of perfection; and we are told that it is only under such a form of government that true liberty and equality of rights can be enjoyed. But an examination of the subject will convince us, that if the working classes of the United Kingdom should obtain any or all of the political changes just mentioned, they would remain in almost the same condition of poverty and ignorance and misery as they are at present. Indeed, all history proves, by the unfailing test of experience, that such would be the case. Let us turn to the records of former ages—let us look at either ancient or modern republics—at all nations, in all times—and inquire if, under any of their varied forms of government and systems of religion, equal rights and equal laws were ever enjoyed! They never were, for such equality is utterly incompatible with inequality of possessions and the gradation of classes—and this state of society has always prevailed. Equality and inequality cannot, from their nature, be reconciled.

The possession of political power by a people, although in accordance with the *principle* of that equality which all good men wish to see established and enjoyed, does not of itself constitute the equality of rights; for although no equality of rights can be enjoyed by a nation without the accompaniment of universal suffrage, yet universal suffrage is neither necessarily accompanied with, nor productive of, equal rights. Equal political power and equal rights are by no means synonymous terms. There is between them all the difference that can exist between a thing and the word by which it is represented.

In considering governmental institutions, we must always judge of their utility by the effects which are seen in connection with them, as we judge of their justness by the principles on which they are established. If the institutions founded on the acknowledgment of human equality be productive of bad effects, and inflict wrong or suffering on any part of the community, it is certain either that the principle of equality is a bad one, or else that it is not allowed pair play. The political institutions of the United States are based on the broad principle of equality of rights; which principle, as it is in accordance with the nature of things, must necessarily be good. But it does not follow that a principle is acted upon, simply because the justice of it is acknowledged. The equality of rights which is thought to be enjoyed by the people of the United States, is so enjoyed only in imagination. There is the same inequality of rights amongst them as amongst us; for they, like ourselves, are divided into rich and poor—into capitalists and producers—and the last are there, as they are here, at the mercy of the first. The class to which the indispensable belong—the working class—is in the same condition throughout the whole world; for society is upon the same principle in all countries; and it is solely from the present social system—from the division of society into employers and employed—into idlers and workers —that the wrongs of the working classes take their rise. The American working men, like the English working men, form a foundation for the whole social pile to rest upon: they are each crushed into the earth by the accumulated weight of an aristocracy and a trading class—by livers on plunder and livers on profit—and as no mere change of government prevents the division of society into these various classes, nor alters the relation in which they stand with regard to each other, all such changes must necessarily fail to correct the evils and wrongs with this division and relation naturally call into existence. The vulture money-monger is the same, whether he be called a monarchist or a republican—the gorge of the one is just as wide and as deep as that of the other.

The citizens of the United States, it is true, are ex-empted, by their republican form of government, from some of the grievous burthens and restrictions which the monar-chical form imposes upon the people of the United King-dom; but these are merely trifles in comparison with that vast social burthen which the working class has sustained in all countries for so many ages,—and even these advan-tages, trivial as they are, will not always be enjoyed by the Americans. Their present exemption arises from the peculiar circumstances by which they are surrounded, in respect to place and to time, and has but little connection with the form of their government. The nascent germ of monarchy exists in the very constitution of American soci-ety—its black and bloody stem is already shooting upwards from the social soil—and it may confidently be predicted, from the common course of events, that the United States republic will merge into a monarchy or an oligarchy before the end of the present century, unless the movement be stopped by a change in the constitution of society. Such has invariably been the ultimate fate of all republics, in ancient and modern times; and such ever must be their fate while one man is rich and another is poor—while one man works and another does nothing.

Tyranny is the same thing throughout the whole world; and it all arises from the same source—the division of society into classes and castes. This all-pervading curse blights alike the happiness of the civilised and the savage man; for in all countries there are what are called superiors and inferiors—the first created to order, and the last to obey. At one time this principle of inequality of rights rears its brazen front in the form of governmental oppression by "right divine," and takes, openly, the lives and the fortunes of the governed: at another time it exists covertly, as it now does in the United States of America, and in Great Britain, and France, where it enables one or two classes of the community to suck into their own substance, unobserved, unceasingly, and unmercifully, the wealth which has been created by the toils and privations of the working class.

This is the great wrong for which a remedy is wanted; and it will shortly be seen that universal suffrage, or even the overthrow of the monarchy and the establishment of a republic, will not be this remedy. There is a stubbornness in facts which theory will in vain strive to overcome; and however much may be admired the justice and excellence of the principles of equality on which the great republic of the west is founded, yet the experience of every day incontestibly proves, that these principles are totally unheeded by the Americans. There are no greater tyrants in existence than the moneyed republicans of the United States. Liberty, and equality of rights, are words which they do not yet know the meaning of; for, apart from the tyranny which the present constitution of society enables one white man to exercise over another, these republicans —in total disregard of their Declaration of Independence, which says that "men are born, and ought always to continue, *free* and *equal* in respect of their rights"—these republicans, disregarding even the appearance of conform-

ing to the spirit of their constitution, now hold in undisguised and abject slavery upwards of two millions of their
coloured fellow-men, who are bought and sold, or flogged
and slain, like cattle. This glaring contradiction between
principle and practice is but a natural result of inequality
of wealth ; and such tyranny and slavery will invariably
be found to exist, either openly or disguisedly—upon black
men or upon white men—in every nation, whatever its
form of government may be, where inequality of possessions
and the division of society into employers and employed
has existence.

If the free institutions of the Americans were acted up
to, no slavery, whether of black men or of white, could
exist in that country. But the spirit of equality, on
which these institutions are founded, is unfelt and unknown by the people,—and why is it so? Because there
are two classes—a class to labour, and a class to *control*
labour—the first poor, and the last rich. The outrage
upon principle—the glaring injustice—there observable, is
produced by the relative situation of the parties; and this
difference of situation originates from, and is maintained by,
the present arrangements of society, —which, independent
of all inequality of mental or physical powers in men, inevitably produce inequality of condition, and divide society
into those who labour and those who set labour in motion,
and thus give the last dominion over the first. The same
iniquitous system prevails not only in the United Kingdom,
but in France, and the European republics, and throughout
the whole world; and that tyranny and slavery should exist
so palpably under the free institutions of the United
States, only tends to enforce still stronger upon us this
indisputable and overwhelming truth,—that neither these
free institutions, nor any other political institutions having
for their object the bestowment of equal rights upon a
people, can be acted up to, or their advantages be universally enjoyed, under our present social arrangements. Slavery
in nature, if not in name, has ever been, is now, and ever
will be, the portion of the working classes, in every country where inequality of property exists in connection with
the gradation of classes.

Let the people of the United Kingdom, then, pause in their
efforts to catch the bubbles which have hitherto charmed
them ; for should they acquire all that they are now strug-

gling for, in respect to the attainment of what are called their
political rights, they will only grasp a shadow—they will
but obtain the letter, not enjoy the spirit, of that great
law of equality of rights which has been instituted by the
Creator. They have before them, as an example of failure,
one of the most enlightened and powerful republics of
ancient or modern times—a nation whose form of government is all that politicians wish for, and far more than the
oppressed people of Britain hope to obtain—and yet this
great nation, in cold-blooded cruelty, and disregard of
human rights, sinks below England herself, king-ridden
and priest-ridden as she has been for centuries!

As, then, sufficient proof is afforded us, by times past
and times present, that no form of government can insure
to a people the enjoyment of equal rights—that no form
of government, whether republican or monarchical, can
protect the productive classes from the exactions and the
tyranny of the useless classes, nor guarantee to the former
the enjoyment of the fruits of their industry—what plan
must be adopted to overthrow and destroy the secret
enemy which devours us?

It requires no arguments to prove that man was
intended, by his Creator, to live in a state of society, or
communion with his kind; and if society, in its present
state, inflicts upon any of its members as many wrongs as
it confers benefits, it cannot from hence be inferred that
the principle of communion is necessarily attended by
these wrongs and sufferings: it is far more rational, and
more in accordance with the perfect adaptation of other
means to other ends, to conclude that we do not act properly upon this principle of communion; for man is much
more likely to err in following, than Nature in directing.

Equality of rights is the very soul of society; but
equality of rights cannot exist unallied with equality of
duties. This is the sum and substance of equality. Thus,
if three men be placed upon a desart island, and they each
give an equal portion of labour for the common good,
and receive an equal reward, the communion is *equally*
beneficial to all the three. But if one of the party, by
force or fraud, obtain *double* allowance of produce for only
single work, the union cannot longer be *equally* beneficial
to all the three. If, again, the same man compel his fellows to give him double allowance of produce for *no labour*

whatever, every shadow of equality and justice vanishes at once ; and no law nor regulation can restore the equilibrium of right, unless it compel this receiver of an unearned share to give his labour for such share ; for the very essence of the inequality and the wrong consists in the inequality of the duties rendered and the rewards received by the several parties. There is no exponent of equal rights but that which also stands for equal duties ; and if duties be unequal, or equal duties be unequally rewarded, the very principle of justice is at once invaded, and equality of rights destroyed.

In all civilised countries, as they are called, society is thus divided into idlers and producers—into those who obtain double allowance for doing nothing, and those who receive only half-allowance for doing double work; and so long as this difference of position and inequality of condition is suffered to exist, inequality of rights and laws and enjoyments will also exist. It matters not how society came to be in its present state. It is sufficient that it is found thus, and that it may be altered and amended. Why *should* some men receive double allowance for doing only single work, or quadruple allowance for rendering no service whatever? All the excessive toil, and poverty, and misery of the working classes of all countries arise solely from this most unjust and iniquitous manner of apportioning the labour and the reward ; and never, until we alter the social arrangements which produce and perpetuate this injustice, can we obtain relief. What arguments are needed to prove to common sense, that, if ten men have to maintain twenty, the ten must work harder or longer than if they had only themselves to keep? What kind of *equality of rights* can there possibly be between the keepers and the kept? There is neither equality of service rendered nor received ; for the one party *gives all,* and the other party *takes all*—and herein lies the essence and spirit of all inequality.

It does not follow, merely because society is now divided into productive and unproductive classes, that the division is either natural or inevitable, as the political economists have asserted. A very cursory examination of the causes which render men rich and poor, and maintain the inequality of condition after it has been created, will shew us that this inequality, so far from being dependent on inequality of bodily and mental powers in individuals, exists in *defiance* of any such inequality of powers, and is in no way connected with these powers—that it arises from causes which no individual can properly command or control, whatever may be the superiority or inferiority of his mental and corporeal faculties.

It may be consistent with the ignorance and the false notions of things which the present social system fosters, to contend for the excellence and the propriety of this system, and to decry all improvement and all change; but those from whom the thick veil of the present has been lifted up—who can survey the bright and the glorious prospect contained within the future—such favoured ones, wherever they may be, will not regard the gross injustice and depravity which now exist in the world, as things intended for perpetuity by an immaculate and perfect Creator.

If the advocates of the present system, with its black catalogue of crimes and vices—if the wealthy and the self-styled high and mighty of the earth—can conceive of no other system, and do not know more of the nature of man than that he may be enslaved and degraded, they know but the half, and the worst half, of his capabilities. Awful, to such, will be the blast of that coming tempest, which the strongest must bend to, and the highest fall down before!

CHAPTER II.

FIRST PRINCIPLES RELATING TO SOCIETY AND GOVERNMENT.

An acquaintance with the first principles of things is the end of all knowledge; and the proper application of these principles is the end of all wisdom. Of all principles, none are of so much importance to man as those which influence and regulate society ; and none are so little inquired into, or so little understood. The false views of himself, his position, and his relation to things, which the present system of society and the contracted education connected with it, compel man to entertain, render it almost impossible for him either to become acquainted with his real nature, or to form any conception of the high destiny which may be his even upon the globe he now inhabits.

Like all other bodies, man is governed by certain principles, or influences, which he obeys necessarily ; and these influences take their rise from the circumstances in which the individual is placed. The various institutions by which man is surrounded, trace out the orbit in which his thoughts, and feelings, and actions are to move ; and on he goes, for centuries, the same old beaten round of crime and folly. Social systems, like solar systems, contain within themselves but few disturbing forces ; and it is the nature of the same institutional circumstances, whether good or bad, to give a general uniformity of character, in respect to actions and opinions, to all who are exposed to their influence. The institutions act upon the man, and the man, in turn, re-acts upon the institutions. Thus the aristocracy of to-day thinks and acts almost the same as aristocracies have always thought and acted ; and the working classes of the present time cringe to their oppressors, and kiss the hand that smites them, the same as their order did three thousand years since.

The world at large have not chosen the present social system, and the particular mode of thinking and acting connected with it, because it was good, nor have they rejected another because it was bad; but men have blindly taken both good and bad, as they happened to turn up, without knowing the one from the other. We of the present day, in like manner, take principles and institutions, and act upon them, simply because they were so taken and acted upon by those who have gone before us. Although a gradual movement is ever going forward, yet society, as a whole, has hitherto had no more inherent power within itself to change at once the direction of its actions and opinions, than have the planets of our solar system a power to change their courses. Whenever a new direction is given to the opinions and pursuits of men, the motion is occasioned by the accumulation of disturbing forces, or by the unwelcome pounce of some cometary spirit on whom no continuity of every-day circumstance has acted,—but whose course, directed by peculiarity of position and singularity of circumstance, lies directly across or against that of the whole of which he forms a part. And when the current of human events is thus broken in upon, it takes necessarily, whether good or bad, the new direction which is given; and this course is maintained until again changed by new influences and new disturbances.

There always have been, in all countries and under all forms of government, individuals in mental advance of, and apparently in opposition to, the main body of a people. They are the pioneers to the march of mind—the first to give battle to prejudice, and the first to fall before it—and, although they make the road to knowledge, to freedom, and to happiness, practicable and easy, they do so only by paving it with their own bones. The vocation of these invaders of the dark empire of ignorance and tyranny renders them the especial dread of despots, and all other upholders of usurped power and unjustly-acquired wealth; and they are therefore always persecuted with a horrible malignancy which no other being but man can feel and exercise.

When we take into consideration the various circumstances which have retarded human advancement, we can-

can be permanently established ; and they naturally suggest a mode of action, in respect to social institutions, which will enable man to enjoy all the pleasures and escape from all the ills which his nature can be cognisant of. It is not rational to suppose that the present inequalities in society must always exist, merely because they exist for the time being ; nor is it in accordance with experience to infer that, because a mode of action is invariable under certain influences and circumstances, it will continue unalterable under all influences and circumstances. Man is man at the pole as well as at the equator, but the diet and the clothing of the one will never be adopted by the other ; nor will the selfish principle exert itself so vilely and so evilly, in a state of society where the rights and the duties of all are equal, as it does under the present social system, where there is no equality either in respect to rights or to duties, to services or to rewards.

That all men are precisely equal in their mental and bodily powers, or that they all require the same quantity of sustenance, no one will attempt to assert ; for absolute equality prevails not between any two created beings. But the inequality of powers which at present exists amongst men, has been induced, in a great degree, by the favourable or unfavourable circumstances in which individuals have been placed, in respect to position in society and means of development ; and, in most cases, if the circumstances and influences had been reversed, the inequality would also have been reversed.

The proud and pampered aristocrat, who has possessed every advantage which circumstances could afford for the development of his tiny brains, possesses, perhaps, knowledge and acquirements which fall not to the son of labour ; but, forgetful of how much circumstances of position have done for him—forgetful that it was the toil and privation of the working man which gave him leisure and means—he tells us, sneeringly and insultingly, that he is a wiser and a higher being than the man whose honest hands procure his bread. But this assumption of superiority has almost had its day, and will soon be neither heeded nor conceded ; and the unnatural barriers which ignorance and fraud have reared to separate men into classes and castes, like cattle in a public market, will be broken through and trodden under foot.

As nature has made the preservation of life dependent on the fulfilment of the same conditions, and has given to every human being the powers adequate to maintain existence, strict equity requires not only that these powers should be duly exercised, but likewise that the exertion should be rewarded with success; and that it is not so rewarded, is not the fault of nature, but of man.   Nature never commits errors—never inflicts injustice; and when she made man the slave of circumstances, and left him at the mercy of events, she gave him faculties adequate to control the one and direct the other.   That he might do this more effectually, and have dominion over most things relating to his existence, man has been taught to institute society; which, if it be wisely regulated, will enable him to accomplish, by a proper union and direction of forces, that which no isolated exertion of human power could ever achieve.   This is the intention and end of society; and the first step to the attainment of the wished-for power is the establishment of institutions which will destroy or neutralise the trifling inequalities that nature has created, and at the same time remove all the uncertainty connected with the future welfare of man, and insure him, until death, an abundance of all those things which make life desirable.   Society, thus constituted and regulated, will draw the whole human family into one common bond of fellowship and union; for its very principles, by showing to all men their dependence on all, prove to them that man has no pre-eminence above his fellow-man; as the wisest and the strongest are but as broken reeds when placed beyond the pale of society, and shut out from the communion and co-operation of their kind.

Thus, from a consideration of the nature of man and the object of society, a principle may be deduced, which, although now unacted upon, and its justice unacknowledged, will ultimately unite the two jagged and far-separated ends of the social chain—forming it into a circle, and putting the last finish upon man and his institutions, namely:—

4. As self-preservation is the end of all labour, and as a general natural equality of powers and wants prevails amongst men, it should follow, that all those who perform *equality of labour* ought likewise to receive *equality of reward.*

However unpalatable may be these principles, they are not only in strict accordance with justice, but they are the only principles capable of destroying the manifold ills and miseries which a departure from them, in the present constitution of society, necessarily engenders.

Some of those who feed upon the produce of the workman's industry, and yield him no service in return, may boldly assert that equality of condition can never have existence; they may endeavour to prove that society is like a human body—that there must be a head, a belly, and members—some to govern and some to obey, some to produce that others may consume. But this simile will not support the cause it is brought to subserve; for all men are of one nature—they are similar powers, or quantities, or qualities—and, as such, there can be no diversity of attributes amongst them. We must liken men to each other, and bellies to each other, and limbs to each other : we cannot compare an arm to a belly or a head, for they are not similar powers, and the one can by no possibility perform the functions of the other, place them in whatever circumstances we may. But what *one man* can do, *another man* may do,—whether it be to rule as king or obey as subject—they are similar powers—and therefore there never can be a natural or a just division of society into belly and members—into mere consumers and producers. All men are of one substance and one nature, they all have the like attributes, and they are all, therefore, equal in respect of their rights.

When we have arrived at the first principles of any thing, we can almost see, as it were, the end of our journey, and have only to march forward upon a straight and open road. We no longer wander about in a labyrinth of doubt and conjecture, perpetually suffering wrongs and devising and rejecting remedies ; but we know exactly where we are, and the course which we ought to pursue. Thus we know that life is dependent upon food, and that food is dependent upon labour. We see at once, that, from the very nature of things, these dependencies are absolute; and that, therefore, if labour be evaded by any human being, it can be thus *evaded by individuals* only on the condition of *increased labour by the mass.* It requires no arguments, when we view for one moment the poor toiler and the rich idler, to prove that the exemp-

tion from labour which the latter enjoys, is attributable to
the inequality of possessions which exists between the two
parties; and it is equally apparent, that inequality of
possessions must have been originally induced, as it is now
partly maintained, by the exclusive possession, by certain
individuals and classes, of that earth which rightly and
equally belongs alike to every created being. Thus the
conviction is naturally and imperatively forced upon us,
that individual possession of the soil has been one cause of
inequality of wealth—that inequality of wealth necessarily
gives rise to inequality of labour—and that inequality of
wealth, and labour, and enjoyments, constitute the wrong
as a whole. This, as well as the deprivation of political
power connected with it, is the state of things to be
remedied; and if the wrong is to be removed, it must be
done by removing the inequality of condition which
creates and perpetuates it. Equality of rights can
never exist in connection with inequality of labour and
inequality of wealth. The mere fact that men have heretofore always been governed by unequal laws—that these
laws have been based on assumed inequality of rights—
and that the idea of inequality of rights has been derived
from inequality of possessions—ought to convince us of the
unimprovable nature of a social system allowing of the
distinctions in society which now exist; for so long as we
hear of rich and poor—of superior and inferior—of master
and man—there can be no equality of rights, no justice,
no cessation of discontent and crime.

From the nature and position of man, and the principles which have relation to his existence, it cannot be
denied that the natural rights of all human beings are
equal. These rights, therefore, can never be given up or
taken away, for they are attributes—conditions of existence—and they are limited, in every man, only by the
equal rights of every other man. Thus, it may be said
that every man has a right to do what he likes—*provided
the so doing interferes not with the* EQUAL *rights of his fellow-man.* This definition, broad as it may appear, is in
reality extremely circumscribed, and will allow neither of
licentiousness nor tyranny. It is an indisputable right of
man to live upon that earth on which he has been placed
by his Creator; and this right to existence must from its
nature be accompanied, in every man, by the right of

appropriating to himself the various necessaries of life which he can, by his labour, compel the earth to yield him. The exercise of these rights, in a well-regulated society, can neither cause collision nor inflict injury; for the acting upon them by one man does not necessarily interfere with the same action on the part of every other man. Human rights must all, and at all times, be tested by this principle of interference; and whenever any man, or body of men, or government, commits an action or makes a claim which interferes with the equal rights of others, a wrong is committed upon all who are thus interfered with.

Men preceded us, and others will continue to come after us. Generations arrive within the confines of existence before their predecessors have departed; and, as the lives of all are held by the same tenure, and are dependent upon the same contingencies, the absolute rights of all to life and sustenance must necessarily be equal. But, from the peculiar position in which we are placed, by the rising and the passing generations being always mixed up together, it is impossible to maintain this natural equality of right to subsistence, unless the earth be COMMON PROPERTY, and the earth cannot be common property, nor can its blessings be either universally or equally enjoyed, under any system which admits individual appropriation of the soil.

It is labour alone which bestows value; for labour, as it has been truly said, is the purchase money which is paid for everything we eat, or drink, or wear. Every man has an undoubted right to all that his honest labour can procure him. When he thus appropriates the *fruits* of his labour, he commits no injustice upon any other human being; for he interferes with no other man's right of doing the same with the produce of *his* labour. But if any individual appropriate to himself the *field* on which all labour is exercised—if he attempt to set up a claim to any particular part of the earth—he clearly does that which is unjust, and contrary to the common equality of rights, *for he interferes with the equal right of every human being to appropriate that same particular spot.* Priority of possession gives no title whatever; nor can any duration of enjoyment establish a right, where a right did not originally exist. From the very nature of the thing, and the position in which man stands with regard to his fellows, he never did, and never can, individually, possess any

exclusive right to one single inch of land.   Wherever such
an assumed right is set up and acted upon, there will
always exist injustice, and tyranny, and poverty, and
inequality of rights, whether the people be under the
monarchical or the republican form of government; for all
the wrongs and the woes which man has ever committed
or endured, may be traced to the assumption of a right in
the soil, by certain individuals and classes, to the exclusion of other individuals and classes.   Equality of rights
can never be enjoyed until all individual claims to landed
property are subverted, and merged in those of the nation
at large.

The next step which man has ever taken, after having
claimed property in land, has been to claim *property in
man ;* and wherever one man possesses land, and another
has none, the latter must always be the slave of the former.
From this prolific source of evil—exclusive possession of
the soil—have arisen semi-civilized despotisms, and governmental power of every description; for an infringement
upon one of the rights of man soon leads to a disregard of
all his other rights.   But we have seen, from the very
nature of things, that no man can ever possess a *right* to
the obedience of another, nor claim property in him; and
therefore, wherever such a pretension is set up, it must be
denounced and resisted, for it is contrary to the letter and
the spirit of Nature's great charter of equality.   The
Creator of man only is the owner of man; and the
assumption of power and dominion by one man or one class
over other men and other classes, simply because the one
claims land and the other does not, is as unjust as the
inequality of property is unjust upon which such claim to
exclusive authority is founded.

Man, as an individual, is both weak and poor, and he
will always continue thus while isolated and alone.   But
he enters society—an aggregate of weak threads produce
a powerful rope—an aggregate of individuals compose a
nation.   If man be weak and poor when left to himself, he
must necessarily continue weak and poor, as an individual,
in any and every state of society ; for society alters neither
his physical constitution nor his attributes—he is still no
more than one thread of the rope.   By what principle,
then, does any individual *claim* power and authority over
his fellows ?   If weakness and insignificance be inherent
in one man, they will likewise be inherent in all men—

they will differ in degree only, not in kind.   A thing is equal to itself, and a whole is greater than its part; and there is nothing in nature or in language that can give us an idea of *one equal* being superior to *another equal*, or greater than a thousand or a million of itself.   Therefore all such assumption of superiority—such toad-blown affectation of supremacy—merits only derision and contempt. There cannot, perhaps, exist a state of society without a form of government and laws of some kind : but there never was, and there never can be, in any person, a *right* to govern ; nor can one individual ever justly make laws for another, and call upon him for obedience.   Human rights are equal ; and human rights are the true foundation for human laws, and the correct definers of man's authority over man.

Laws, if properly considered, are no more than contrivances to promote the welfare of society ; and therefore they should be so framed as to afford the greatest security to the whole body politic, with the least restraint upon the actions of individuals.   Such being the nature and intention of laws, it is evident that all those must be both prejudicial and unjust, which tend to circumscribe the rights of individuals, without at the same time affording additional protection to the community.   With respect to the institution of laws, *no minority can ever possess the* RIGHT *of imposing laws upon the majority* ; and therefore, wherever laws have been thus imposed, a manifest tyranny has been committed upon the majority.   Nor can a majority ever possess the right of imposing laws upon the minority, except such laws have for their object the *equal protection of general social rights ;* for the protection of persons and property being the chief end for which men institute laws—and as every man who respects the rights of others, ought also to have his own rights held sacred—it follows, that all laws instituted by either majority or minority, *for such equal protection of rights,* are binding upon all. But if, from ignorance of the nature of right, or from any other cause, the majority or minority think fit to enact laws which *interfere with the rights of all* without at the same time affording *equal protection to all,* they clearly do that which is unjust.   Of this indefensible and tyrannical character are the laws now existing in England and other countries, which, under pain of fine or imprisonment, render it compulsory *on all persons* to perform certain religious observances on a stated day.   In regard to England, these laws were enacted by an insignificant minority of the nation ; but had they been passed with the consent of the majority, they would have been equally unjust and tyrannical in principle, and equally worthy of detestation and resistance ; for they trespass upon the right of one part of the nation to enjoy their free will in the matter, without affording any additional protection to the other part.   Those who enacted the laws, not only protected their own right to perform certain services—which no one could dispute—but they, at the same time, infringed on the equal rights of others *to dispense with their observance.* There is not one law in existence in Great Britain, which is not more or less contaminated by this tyrannical principle of interference with private and public right, under the guise of protecting such right.

The rights of man, from their very nature, are independent of, and unconnected with, majorities and minorities ; for such can neither give them nor take them away. From the very principle of equality by which they are regulated, it must follow, that the natural rights of any aggregation of individuals cannot outweigh the rights of a single individual ; and although any nation, or combination of men, have an undoubted right to institute any laws they please *relating to themselves,* yet such laws cannot justly operate upon any non-consenting party, except the principle of equality of rights be invaded by such party.

All the forms of government at present existing are in a greater or less degree tyrannical and irresponsible.   The wrongs which emanate from them operate upon the people, generally, in an indirect manner, through the medium of laws ; and such laws are always necessarily imbued with the spirit of inequality which pervades the government from which they spring.   Might and Right have long been, with rulers, synonymous terms ; and right and wisdom and virtue are supposed to be inherent in certain persons and classes of the community, independent of other persons and classes.   But all these ideas of superior and inferior—of master and man—may be traced to the neglect of First Principles, and to the consequent rise of inequality of possessions ; and such ideas will never be eradicated, nor the institutions founded upon them be subverted, so long as this inequality is maintained.   Men have hitherto blindly hoped to remedy the present unna-

tural state of things, and to institute equality of rights
and laws, by removing one rich tyrant and setting up
another—by destroying *existing inequality*, and leaving
untouched the *cause* of the inequality ; but it will shortly
be seen, that it is not in the nature of any mere governmental change to afford permanent relief—that misgovernment is not a cause, but a consequence—that it is not the
creator, but the created—*that it is the offspring of inequality of possessions ;* and that inequality of possessions is
inseparably connected with our present social system.
From this it will follow, that the present state of things
cannot be remedied, unless we change at once our whole
social system ; for, alter our form of government as we
will, no such change can affect the system—no such change
can prevent inequality of possessions, and the division of
society into employers and employed—and therefore, as a
necessary consequence, no such change can remove the
evils which this system and this division of society engender.

We do not act, and never yet have acted, upon those
First Principles which the Creator has instituted for the
guidance and the welfare of man ; nor do we keep the
broad principle of equality in view, either in our rights or
our duties, our labours or our rewards. With us, almost
everything is unequal, and unnatural, and unjust. And
why are things thus ? How is it that some men receive
only half allowance for doing double work, while others
receive double or quadruple allowance merely for looking
on ? There is no principle in numbers which will make
one man to be fifty, or a hundred—there is no principle in
production which will enable one unaided man, with
powers only equal to those of any other man, to perform
the united labour of one hundred—and there is no principle of reason or of justice which will allow one man to
appropriate the fruits of the labour of one hundred. And
yet this unjust appropriation has been practised and tolerated, in defiance of every principle of numbers and of
justice, from the creation of man to the present day.
Such is the operation of the present social system—on
fraud and robbery legalised stand all its power, and wealth,
and glory—and until this system be overthrown, and the
immutable principles of truth established, let no man
speak of peace, or look for justice, or hope for happiness !

CHAPTER III.

THE CONDITIONS REQUISITE FOR INDIVIDUAL AND
NATIONAL PROSPERITY.

WERE we, apart from the feelings and the prejudices which conventional and educational circumstances have impressed upon us, to take a survey of the whole human family, we might compare them to shipwrecked men, thrown upon an almost desert island.   There is sufficient room for all to live and move, and plenty of the mere elements of everything necessary to support existence ; but nothing can be done without labour. It requires labour to gather even the wild fruits from the trees, or the shell-fish from the sea-shore.   Without labour, we die.

Surely, the most rational mode of action for men so circumstanced would be, to unite together in parties, work and share alike, and render to each other mutual assistance and protection ; for, by acting thus, the labour of each person would be infinitely lightened, and his security be much increased.   The strong could defend the weak, and the wary advise the strong : all might be of service.

But men have heretofore done nothing of the kind. The motto of almost every member of the human family has been, and still is—" Each for himself." We have pursued different tracks, and have moved on alone, although we have all been in search of the same object. —an object, too, which could by no possibility be obtained by one man except through the instrumentality of his fellows.   We have been weak when we might have been strong—we have been naked and hungry when we might have been clothed and fed—we have been bitter and im-placable enemies when we might have been kind and sted-fast friends.

We have suffered and sinned thus on account of our ignorance, and our inattention to First Principles. No common bond of sympathy and fellow-feeling has ever drawn the hearts of men together, for there has been among them no common interest. We have always left both the end and the means to chance—to uncontrolled circumstance—which has apportioned to each man his labours, and his rewards, and his punishments, almost independent of either capability, or exertion, or desert. One man has found an oyster and another has met with a shell—one man has been filled to repletion, and another has starved.

This chance-way of maintaining life, although it may be agreeable to the nature of brutes, was never intended to be acted upon by rational beings. Notwithstanding that we have ever claimed superiority over all other earthly beings—and have assumed such pre-eminence solely on account of our reason—yet hitherto, in respect to our social institutions, we have made little or no use of this great distinctive attribute. Man has a reasonable as well as an instinctive nature—each given him as a means to attain a certain end—and each being intended to accomplish that which the other cannot effect. When man grovels among the instincts, he has no pre-eminence above a beast—he becomes not man until he reasons, and obeys the dictates of that reason.

The present social system is based upon the instinctive, and not the reasonable, nature of man. It gives development and strength only to our brute perceptions and propensities. It leaves our self-love to be guided by our instinct instead of by our reason, in the formation of institutions ; and consequently, as the instinct of man is less perfect than that of any other animal, so is the state of society founded upon that instinct more imperfect than the community which nature has taught the very bees and beavers to institute. Man has ever been in an unnatural position ; and therefore, of necessity, he has always been unhappy or discontented—always seeking for change. This restlessness—this eternal yearning after we know not what—is not an inherent principle or faculty in man, which must operate in all circumstances and under all influences ; for, had this universally prevalent discontent been rightly reasoned upon, and analysed, it would have been found to proceed,—not from the nature of man, and the incompetency of earthly things to make him happy—but from the unnatural position in which man has ever existed with respect to his fellows, and the little use and ill use which he has made of his higher faculties.

Unhappiness is not felt by any created being, so long as such being is in the position which nature intended it to occupy ; and it is manifested equally by all, when removed from such position. The Creator intended all creatures to be happy, and therefore placed them in proper situations, or gave them attributes and faculties calculated for their preservation and enjoyment. Experience teaches us, that if we remove any animal from its proper position into one alien to its nature, it immediately exhibits all that rest-lessness and discontentment which has so long been the characteristic of man. Man now exists in an unnatural state—as an instinctive rather than a rational being—and he is therefore necessarily restless and dissatisfied ; and so he must remain, until he alters his position. Shall we, then, by the aid of those gigantic powers which we possess, create around us circumstances congenial to our nature, and thus become contented and joyful ; or shall we stupidly continue to tax the Great Giver of life—that Almighty Power whose every law is immutably just—with partiality or tyranny ?   Let us cease our maudlin lamentations, and our outcries, that we only, in a universe of adaptation and perfectibility, are lost and forsaken and miserable beings. Let us, for once, make some use of our much-boasted but much-neglected reason ; and take that station—create those circumstances—fulfil that end—for which existence was bestowed upon us.

The poverty and misery of the masses of all nations have for ages been notorious. It was easy to make the oppressed believe, ere Mind had touched them with its quickening spark, that their condition in society, as the slaves and the inferiors of their fellow-men, was a necessary consequence of their existence, and therefore unavoidable and irremediable. But, as time progressed, knowledge spread ; and the sons of labour began not only to disbelieve the story of their inferiority, but likewise to attempt to throw off the yoke of the merciless enemy which had so long held them in thraldom. The frequent and vigorous efforts which have been made for this purpose during the last half-century, have not been unheeded by the opposite party; and they have discovered the necessity of supporting their pretensions to supremacy and wealth by stronger proof than mere assertion. To this end have certain individuals examined the ground-work and tendency of the existing system; and their labours have ended in the erection of what is called the science of Political Economy. The founders of this science have gone to first principles—they have reasoned from indisputable facts—and they have proved, clearly and convincingly, that, under the present system, there is no hope for the working man—that he is indeed the bondman of the man of money—and that he is kept so by circumstances which neither his enemy nor himself can immediately control.

But let not the unjust man and the extortioner, wherever he may be, exult in the immensity of his wealth and the unconquerableness of his power—let not a toil-worn and an impoverished people, wherever they may be, think that their doom is fixed, and that deliverance will never come. That which is true of particular principles under certain influences, is not necessarily true of the same principles under all circumstances; nor is that degradation and poverty, which is the portion of the working man under the present social system, a necessary concomitant of his existence under any and every social system. This shall be proved by the same principles and the same mode of argument by which the political economists, from not going far enough, have proved the contrary. By thus fighting them upon their own ground, and with their own weapons, we shall avoid that senseless clatter respecting "visionaries" and "theorists," with which they are so ready to assail all who dare move one step from that beaten track which, "by authority," has been pronounced to be the only right one. Before the conclusions arrived at by such a course of proceeding can be overthrown, the economists must unsay or disprove those established truths and principles on which their own arguments are founded.

"Society," it has been affirmed by a political economist, "both in its rudest form, and in its most refined and complicated relations, is nothing but a system of exchanges. An exchange is a transaction in which both the parties who make the exchange are benefited;—and, consequently society is a state presenting an uninterrupted succession of advantages for all its members."

It has been to make society what it is here represented to be—"an uninterrupted succession of advantages for ALL its members"—that the efforts of the truly great and good in all ages have been directed. Society *is not* thus universally advantageous to all within its pale, nor has it ever yet been so. Ask the producers of wealth—the despised, the toil-worn, the oppressed working men, of any age or any nation,—if society was ever for them an " uninterrupted succession of advantages." Could their voices arise from the grave—could they tell us the sicken-ing tale of their wrongs and their miseries—how wild would be their wailings !—how terrible their impreca-tions ! But even were history silent as to their fate, experience is a perpetual remembrancer to the men of the present day ; and they cannot change their situation for a better one, nor will they ever have a proper hold upon society, until First Principles are universally acted upon—until we attend to those conditions which the political economists themselves have confessed to be " necessary for the production of Utility, or of what is essential to the support, comfort, and pleasure of human life ;"—and these conditions are :—

" 1. *That there shall be labour.*

" 2. *That there shall be accumulations of former labour, or capital.*

" 3. *That there shall be exchanges.*"

These three conditions, be it remembered, are those laid down by the economists. There is no reservation made—no distinction of any particular persons or classes with respect to whom these conditions shall or shall not have reference. They are applied to society at large, and, from their nature, cannot exempt any individual or any class from their operation. We must, therefore, take the conditions as they are, and apply them, with their advan-tages and their disadvantages, to all alike.

Had these conditions been fulfilled by men, as they ought to have been, there would now be no occasion for forming associations to obtain political rights, or trades' unions to protect the employed from the merciless exac-tions of the employers. But these conditions have been neglected, or only partially observed, and the present con-

dition of the working man and society at large is the consequence. From our habits and prejudices, it is difficult
to discover truths or First Principles, but it is still more
difficult to apply these principles properly, or even to conceive that they may be acted upon. First Principles are
always general in their application—not partial. The
ban—" THOU SHALT LABOUR"—rests alike on all created
beings. To this great law, from the minutest animalcule
in a drop of water, to the most stupendous whale which
dives beneath the waves of ocean, there are naturally, and
there should be artificially, no exceptions. Man only can
escape this law ; and, from its nature, it can be evade l by
one man only at the expense of another. The law itself
is never destroyed or abrogated—it naturally and perpetually presses equally upon all men—upon the capitalist as
well as the working man—and if one man or one class
escape its pressure, the sum total of its force will bear
up some other man or class. It is an absolute condition of
existence " that there shall be labour."

The word " Labour," with most men, has unpleasant
ideas associated with it. To many, it signifies raggedness,
or ignorance, or degradation—aching bones, mental and
bodily lassitude, a gnawing dissatisfaction with every thing
around them, and a half-weariness of life. To destroy the
inexplicable feelings which excessive labour thus creates,
the over-wrought working man wants, and he must have,
some mental or bodily restorative to supply this waste of
vital energy. But the present institutions of society offer
him nothing of the kind. There is nothing around him to
raise up his prostrated soul, and enlarge and purify the
noble germ within him ; for everything he hears and sees
and feels, tends to enforce upon him a sense of inferiority
and abasement. No wonder that his manhood droops and
withers—that he seeks for the momentary relaxation
afforded by debauchery—that he soon loses even the desire
to improve his very few hours of leisure, and becomes content to plod through life, not as a man, but as an animal—
eating, drinking, and working, to the end of his days.
The almighty principle of Mind, if unused and unim-
proved, sickens, and degenerates, and dies.

Labour, like everything else, is good when used legiti-
mately, but becomes prejudicial when abused. It has
hitherto been regarded as a curse—and it has to many

been an actual curse—only because men have not used it
rightly. The great mass of mankind has laboured to
excess ; and, like every other excess, labour has excited
little else than aversion and loathing.

Labour ought to raise none of these unpleasant emotions ; nor would it do so if taken in moderation. If we
understood things rightly, we should consider labour a
blessing rather than a curse, for it is the one great pre-
servative of intellectual and corporeal health. But, with
strange inattention to the nature and uses of things, the
world at large stamps labour, which is the parent of every
enjoyment, as not only unpleasant, but derogatory. The
working man must not sit with the idler or the capitalist,
nor must he eat with them, or associate with them. The
pot-house and the hovel are allotted to the one—the ball-
room and the palace are usurped by the other. To have
ever honestly earned a shilling, is, under the present
system, and by those who have perched themselves upon
the pinnacles of that system, considered almost as a moral
stain upon a man, which can be wiped away only by
successive generations of idlers. Those are now the most
regarded who can point back to the longest list of ancestors who never did one useful thing, and who have therefore lived for ages upon the industry of the productive
classes, by what can only be called tolerated robbery. But
all labour must come from some parties ; and the advocate
for justice and for equal rights cannot but exclaim—" Let
those only cry out against working who can live without
eating and drinking, for none but such were intended to be
idle."

Labour is neither more nor less than labour ; and one
kind of employment is not more honourable or dishonour-
able than another, although all descriptions of labour may
not appear of equal value to society at large. Such
inequality of value, however, is no argument for inequality
of rewards ; and when we have examined the subject in all
its bearings and relations, we shall find that it is as just
and reasonable that equal labour of all kinds should be
equally remunerated, as it is just and reasonable that
labour should be universal. Man, properly constituted,
requires not the low stimulant of superior pecuniary reward
to spur him on to do his duty to his fellow-man.

All kinds of labour are so mixed up together, and so

dependent on each other that the institution of inequality of rewards involves more actual pecuniary injustice than can possibly have existence under a system which rewards all men and all trades alike, for a similar application of labour ; whilst the moral and physical evils which experi-. ence has proved to be inseparable from the present system of inequality—the uncharitableness, the insatiable greedi-ness, the bloodshed, the wrongs of every kind which the records of three thousand years are filled with—can have little or no existence in connection with equality of reward for equal labour.

Not only are the greatest advantages, but strict justice also, on the side of a system of equality. It must be con-fessed by all men, that the most important discovery or invention, unless labour be applied to bring forth its results, is just as useless to us as the merest trifle. Thus, although it may be said that he who invents a steam-engine confers a greater benefit upon society than the man who makes it,—and that he who makes it does a greater service than he who merely fills it with water and kindles the fire under it,—yet, in reality, the labour of the last man is just as necessary, to produce the effects desired, as the labour of the first. The drawing or model of the inventor is of no value until seconded by the labour of the engine-maker ; and the perfected engine, until it be put in motion by fire and water, is as worthless as the mere model. The results to be produced by the instrumentality of the engine are thus dependent, and equally dependent, upon the labour of all the parties concerned. Every man is a link, and an indispensable link, in the chain of effects —the beginning of which is but an idea, and the end, per-haps, the production of a piece of cloth. Thus, although we may entertain different feelings towards the several parties, it does not follow that one should be better paid for his labour than another. The inventor will ever receive, in addition to his just pecuniary reward, that which genius only can obtain from us—the tribute of our admiration.

Under the present social system, with its individualized and opposing interests, and its high and low employments, equal remuneration for equal labour would be both im-practicable and unjust. Some professions and trades, to obtain a mastery over them, require quadruple the time and expense which are necessary to be devoted to others. Such time and expense are now borne by isolated individuals ; and therefore, as the time and labour attendant on the acquisition of particular employments are so unequal, equal remuneration would involve a positive injustice. But under a rational system of communion and co-operation, where society at large would take upon itself the education and employment of all its members—bear every expense connected with the acquisition of scientific attainments and common trades—and derive, in gross, the peculiar advantages dependant upon the merely momentary unproductiveness of scientific pursuits—equal remuneration for equal labour would be as just towards the inventor of a steam-engine, as towards the maker of the engine, or the man who sets it in motion. Under such a system, containing institutions furnished with every necessary apparatus for investigation and discovery, thousands of persons could easily obtain that scientific knowledge, and enter upon that wide field of experimental research, which it now demands a fortune to acquire and pursue ; and equal remuneration for equal labour would be the true and the just recompense for all services.

In the second place, " *There shall be accumulations of former labour, or capital.*"

We all know that accumulations are no more than the unconsumed products of former labour,—whether houses, machinery, ships, or anything else that is useful, or that can assist us in creating more wealth. All these things are capital. Had the first and succeeding generations of men consumed all that they produced—had they left their successors neither houses, tools, nor any other kind of wealth—we should now necessarily have been, as they were, half-starved and half-clothed savages. It is in the power of every generation, even under the most unfavourable circumstances, to leave the world richer, in respect to accumulations, than they found it ; and it is their duty so to do. The principle of accumulating or saving seems to be instinctive in man, for it has never yet been entirely lost sight of, although it has been acted upon ignorantly, and with little or no knowledge of the important results connected with its fulfilment. We have inherited the greater part of our present accumulation from preceding generations, and merely hold them as it were in trust, for the benefit of ourselves and our successors; for the men of the future have as good a title to them as we have. Every generation thus receives a greater or less amount of accumulated wealth from those which preceded it; therefore, in equity, every generation is bound to provide for its successors in at least the same ratio as itself was provided for; and as population is ever on the increase, so likewise ought accumulations to be always on the increase.

That which applies to a generation, as a whole, applies also to every individual of such generation; and as there ought to be national accumulation, there ought likewise to be individual accumulation, for the first is dependent upon the last. The political economists, with the cold-blooded and calculating voracity induced by the present system, tell the productive classes that they must accumulate— that they must depend upon their own exertions; but however good the advice may be in principle, it is, while the working man is pressed into the earth by existing usages, no more than the addition of an insult to an injury. They *cannot* accumulate; and the reason is,—not because they are idle, not because they are intemperate, not because they are ignorant,—but because those accumulations, which have been handed down for the benefit of the *present generation as a whole,* are usurped, and their advantages exclusively enjoyed, by *particular individuals and classes.*

The third and last condition of the economists is, " *That there shall be exchanges.*"

An exchange is defined to be a transaction between two parties, in which each gives to the other something which he has not so much desire for, as he has for the article which he receives in return. Thus every man who works for hire exchanges his labour for a certain sum of money, because he would rather work, and receive the money, than remain idle, and starve. The capitalist, in like manner, would rather give his money for a certain quantity of labour, than live upon it as long as it should last; for he sells or exchanges the produce of such labour for a greater sum than the labour originally costs him, and by these means is enabled not only to live in idleness, but to increase his store of wealth at the same time. The capitalists, as we have seen, call this species of exchange " a transaction in which *both* the parties who make the exchange are benefited; consequently, society is a state presenting an uninterrupted succession of advantages for *all* its members."

The subject of exchanges is one on which too much attention cannot be bestowed by the productive classes; for it is more by the infraction of this third condition by the capitalist, than by all other causes united, that inequality of condition is produced and maintained, and the working man offered up, bound hand and foot, a sacrifice upon the altar of Mammon.

From the very nature of labour and exchange, strict justice not only requires that all exchangers should be *mutually*, but that they should likewise be *equally*, benefited. Men have only two things which they can exchange with each other, namely, labour, and the produce of labour; therefore, let them exchange as they will, they merely give, as it were, labour for labour. If a just system of exchanges were acted upon, the value of all articles would be determined by the entire cost of production; *and equal values should always exchange for equal values.* If, for instance, it take a hatter one day to make a hat, and a shoemaker the same time to make a pair of shoes— supposing the material used by each to be of the same value—and they exchange these articles with each other, they are not only mutually but equally benefited: the advantage derived by either party cannot be a disadvantage to the other, as each has given the same amount of labour, and the materials made use of by each were of equal value. But if the hatter should obtain *two* pair of shoes for *one* hat—time and value of material being as before—the exchange would clearly be an unjust one. The hatter would defraud the shoemaker of one day's labour; and were the former to act thus in all his exchanges, he would receive, for the labour of *half a year*, the product of some other person's *whole year*; therefore the gain of the first would necessarily be a loss to the last.

We have heretofore acted upon no other than this most unjust system of exchanges—the workmen have given the capitalist the labour of a whole year, in exchange for the value of only half a year—and from this, and not from the assumed inequality of bodily and mental powers in individuals, has arisen the inequality of wealth and power which at present exists around us. It is an inevitable

condition of inequality of exchanges—of buying at one price
and selling at another—that capitalists shall continue to
be capitalists, and working men be working men—the one
a class of tyrants and the other a class of slaves—to
eternity. By equality of exchanges, 'however, no able-
bodied individual can exist, as thousands now do, unless he
fulfil that condition of the economist, " that there shall be
labour ;" nor can one class appropriate the produce of the
labour of another class, as the capitalists now appropriate
and enjoy the wealth which the powers of the working
man daily call into existence. It is inequality of exchanges
which enables one class to live in luxury and idleness, and
dooms another to incessant toil.

By the present unjust and iniquitous system, exchanges
are not only *not* mutually beneficial to all parties, as the
political economists have asserted, but it is plain, from the
very nature of an exchange, that there is, in most transactions between the capitalist and the producer, *after the
first remove,* no *exchange* whatever. An exchange implies
the giving of one thing for another. But what is it that
the capitalist, whether he be manufacturer or landed proprietor, gives in exchange for the labour of the working
man ? The capitalist gives no labour, for he does not
work—he gives no capital, for his store of wealth is being
perpetually augmented. It is certain that the capitalist
can have only his labour or his capital to exchange against
the labour of the working man ; and if, as we daily see,
the capitalist gives no labour, and his original stock of
capital does not decrease, he cannot in the nature of things
make an exchange with anything that belongs to himself.
The whole transaction, therefore, plainly shews that the
capitalists and proprietors do no more than give the
working man, for his labour of one week, a part of the
wealth which they obtained from him the week before !—
which just amounts to giving him *nothing* for *something*—
and is a method of doing business which, however consonant with the established usages of the present system, is
by no means compatible with a working man's ideas of
justice. The wealth which the capitalist appears to give
in exchange for the workman's labour was generated
neither by the labour nor the riches of the capitalist, but
it was originally obtained by the labour of the workman ;
and it is still daily taken from him, by a fraudulent

system of unequal exchanges. The whole transaction, therefore, between the producer and the capitalist, is a palpable deception, a mere farce: it is, in fact, in thousands of instances, no other than a barefaced though legalised robbery, by means of which the capitalists and proprietors contrive to fasten themselves upon the productive classes, and suck from them their whole substance.

Those who assist not in production can never justly be exchangers, for they have nothing on which to draw, and therefore nothing which they can exchange. No man possesses any natural and inherent wealth within himself —he has merely *a capability of labouring ;* therefore, if a man possess any created wealth—any capital—and have never made use of this capability, and have never laboured, the wealth which he holds in possession cannot rightly belong to him. It must belong to some persons who have created it by labour ; for capital is not self-existent. The vast accumulations now in Great Britain, therefore—as they are neither the production of the labour of the present race of capitalists nor their predecessors, and were never given to them in exchange for any such labour—do not belong to the capitalists either on the principle of creation or the principle of exchange. Nor are they theirs by right of heirship ; for having been produced nationally, they can only justly be inherited by the nation as a whole. Thus, view the matter as we will, there is to be seen no towering pile of wealth that has not been scraped together by rapacity—no transaction between the man of labour and the man of money, that is not characterised by fraud and injustice.

Here, then, is demonstration, flowing naturally from facts, that the three great conditions which the economists acknowledge to be "necessary to the support, comfort, and pleasure of human life," are almost unheeded, and two of them totally unacted upon, by the capitalists themselves. The law which says "There shall be labour," is evaded by them : the law which says "There shall be accumulations," is only half fulfilled, and is made to subserve the interests of a particular class, to the detriment of all the rest of the community : the law which says "There shall be exchanges," is not and cannot be observed, on the part of the capitalists, so long as they neglect the law of labour ; for, unless they themselves labour by assisting in production, they can have nothing to exchange. Thus the infraction of these three conditions, by any one class, renders it morally and physically impossible that society should be what it ought to be—" an uninterrupted succession of advantages for all its members." Until these laws are made to operate equally and imperatively upon every part of the community, society must inevitably be what it is now, and what it always has been—an uninterrupted succession of wrongs, and spoliations, and oppressions—a system of perpetual warfare between man and man, under the denomination of employer and employed, in which the last must suffer all the hardship and make good all the damage. The very principles that have been laid down by the political economists incontestibly prove, when we consider the manner in which these principles are acted upon by capitalists and producers, that the interests of the two parties are *not* identified, as those who plunder the working man would have him to believe. The two interests can never be identified—the gain of the employer will never cease to be the loss of the employed—until the exchanges between the parties are equal; and exchanges never can be equal while society is divided into capitalists and producers—the last living upon their labour, and the first bloating upon the profit of that labour.

It is plain, then, from a review of the causes which have produced the present state of things, that, establish whatever form of government we will—possess whatever merely political power we will—there never can be equality of rights and laws amongst us, nor amongst the people of any other nation, so long as the institutions and usages of society make the gain of one man to depend upon the loss of another; and place one class, by its position, at the mercy of another class. We may talk of morality and brotherly love, and of doing as we would be done by; but it is certain that men can never dwell together in unity, and love each other as brethren, unless they have one common end in view, and there be amongst them a perfect reciprocity of benefits; and it is equally certain that no such reciprocity can exist where there are unequal exchanges, and inequality of rewards for equal services.

The great mass of the productive classes look to universal suffrage, or the institution of a republic, as the grand remedy for their wrongs; but it has been shewn that these wrongs arise from a deeper source than form of government, and that they cannot be removed by any mere governmental change. Under the present social system, the whole of the working class are dependent upon the capitalist or employer for the means of labour; and where one class, by its position in society, is thus dependent upon another class for the MEANS OF LABOUR, it is dependent, likewise, for the MEANS OF LIFE; and this is a condition so contrary to the very intention of society—so revolting to reason, to justice, to natural equality of rights—that it cannot for one moment be palliated or defended.   It confers on man a power which ought to be vested in nothing mortal.   Inequality of possessions give man this dominion over his fellow-man; and therefore inequality of possessions, and not particular forms of government, constitute the great evil:—and inequality of exchanges, as being the cause of inequality of possessions, is the secret enemy that devours us.   No simple governmental change can affect the present social system — can alter the relative position of the employer and the employed—can have any influence on inequality of condition; therefore all such changes are illusory, however extensive they may appear; and must, from their nature, be utterly worthless, except in so far as they concern the personal liberty of the governed.   Under a state of things like that which now exists, the working classes, no matter what may be their intelligence, or their morality, or their industry, or their political power—are, by the very constitution of society, and their position in it, doomed and damned to hopeless and irremediable slavery until the end of the world!

CHAPTER IV.

THE CONSEQUENCES OF NEGLECTING FIRST PRIN-CIPLES.

~~~~~~~~~~~~~~~~~~~~~~~~~~~~~~~~~~~~~

It has been shewn by the economists themselves, that three conditions are absolutely necessary to the existence of human society; namely, that there shall be labour—that there shall be accumulations of the produce of labour, or capital—and that there shall be exchanges. It has likewise been demonstrated, that these conditions, from their very nature, and the relation in which men in society stand with regard to each other, can be evaded by one individual or one class, only at the expense of other individuals or classes; and it follows, therefore, that every man commits a wrong upon some part of the community, if he render not to society an equivalent equal to the benefits which he receives. It has been deduced, also, from a consideration of the intention and end of society, not only that all men should labour, and thereby become exchangers, but that equal values should always exchange for equal values—and that, as the gain of one man ought never to be the loss of another, value should ever be determined by cost of production. But we have seen, that, under the present arrangements of society, all men do not labour—that all exchangers, therefore, are not equally benefited—that the gain of the capitalist and the rich man is always the loss of the workman—that this result will invariably take place, and the poor man be left entirely at the mercy of the rich man, under any and every form of government, so long as there is inequality of exchanges—and that equality of exchanges can be insured only under social arrangements in which labour is univer-

sal, and where the remuneration is as equal to the labour.
A few more examples of the working of the present
system will shew us, more clearly, the utter fatuity of
attempting to remedy evils which are inherent in the very
constitution of society, in any other manner than by
a complete reconstruction of the social system.

There are in the United Kingdom, at the present
moment, many thousands of persons who have toiled hard
all their lives, and yet who are not possessed of property of
the value of one year's labour ; and there are also many
thousands who have never performed one month's labour,
and who, nevertheless, are now possessed of wealth of the
value of many hundreds of pounds sterling.   How came
these rich men in possession of this capital?   They have
never laboured, and yet they are not only enabled to live
without working, but their wealth increases every year.
Some of them will tell us—and they glory in the confession—that their property was acquired in by-gone
times, by conquest ; others say that their riches are the
hoarded fruits of their own industry,—meaning, thereby,
the interest or profit which they have obtained by means
of unequal exchanges in the employment of capital ; and
others, again, merely affirm that the wealth which they
possess has been derived from their ancestors, by inherit-
ance.

The attainment of wealth by conquest is so glaringly
unjust, that all claims founded upon it stand self-con-
demned at once ; and that any individual has a right to
take to himself, or to grant to another, one single foot of
earth, has been denied and disproved already,—for the
earth is the common property of all its inhabitants, and
each one has a just claim, not to a particular part of the
earth itself, but merely to that wealth which his labour
can compel the earth to yield him.

Those capitalists who profess to have acquired their
riches by deriving a profit from capital, through the
instrumentality of unequal exchanges, have a claim but one
degree more just than the claim by conquest.   Our daily
experience teaches us, that if we take a slice from a loaf,
the slice never grows on again : the loaf is but an accumulation of slices, and the more we eat of it, the less will
there remain to be eaten.   Such is the case with the loaf
of the working man ; but that of the capitalist follows

not this rule. His loaf continually increases instead of diminishing: with him, it is cut and come again, for ever. Every workman knows that if he save a few pounds sterling, and come to be ill, or out of employment, he can live only for a certain time upon this money. It is his capital—the accumulated produce of his own industry— and it dwindles away until the whole is consumed. And so, likewise, if exchanges were equal, would the wealth of the present capitalists gradually go from them to the working classes: every shilling that the rich man spent, would leave him a shilling less rich ; for from the nature of things it must follow, that if a part be taken from a whole, that which remains must, as a whole, be less than it was before such part was taken from it.

With respect to the acquisition of wealth by inherit-ance, it requires but little reflection to convince us, that past circumstances have rendered it impossible for any member of the productive class to have accumulated, by the most incessant hoarding of the produce of his own industry, wealth amounting to one-fiftieth part of such vast accumulations as so many thousands of individual capitalists and proprietors now hold. It is evident, when we take all things into consideration, that it would require the handing down of the savings of many generations of a working man's family, to amount to the sum even of one thousand pounds sterling; and that this could be done only by a combination of favourable circumstances such as would not have fallen to the lot of one family in a million. We all know that there have been bloody and extermi-nating wars in all ages—that most countries, and Great Britain amongst the rest, have at times been overrun and plundered by bands of armed robbers, and consequently all production of wealth been at a stand—that the produc-tive classes alone, through the medium of unequal exchanges, have always had to support the pride and the pomp of aristocracy and its plaything governments—so that it is all but impossible that any capitalist can have derived even one thousand pounds sterling from the actual hoarded labour of his working-class progenitors.

From the very conditions laid down by the political economists—that there shall be labour, and accumulations, and exchanges—it follows, that there can be no exchanges without accumulations—*no accumulations without labour.*

This latter condition alone condemns at once the cause of the capitalist, and shews the injustice and worthlessness of the tenure by which he holds his wealth. There are accumulations, and therefore there has been labour on the part of certain individuals or certain classes. If the capitalists have created the accumulations they hold, the accumulations are theirs by right of creation; and, if they have obtained them by exchanging for them other accumulations of equal value, then are they theirs by right of exchange. But the great mass of capitalists and proprietors have never laboured in the business of production; and even had they been labourers, they could not have created the wealth in their possession; for their physical and intellectual power, and their consequent capability of production, is not superior to that of the great body of working men. How comes it to pass, then, that he who is idle is rich, while those who are industrious toil on in perpetual poverty? How is it that the wealth of the working man remains stationary, or decreases, while that of the capitalist yearly increases? How is it that the rising man of profit rides upon his horse while the workman walks—the horse gives place to the gig—the gig is superseded by the chariot—and as the rich man grows more rich, he grows more lazy, and performs less work? The anomaly, and the wrong connected with it, we have seen, arises solely from unequal exchanges; for as, under the present system, every working man gives to an employer at least six days' labour for an equivalent worth only four or five days' labour, the gains of the last man are necessarily the losses of the first man. Every fortune, therefore, acquired under this system by means of trade—every accumulation of the capitalists or employers, as a body—is derived from the unsurrendered earnings of the working class, or persons employed; and wherever one man thus becomes rich, he does so only on condition that many men shall remain poor. All men cannot be rich, in the common acceptation of the term; but there is no necessity for one human being to be poor.

Thus, in whatever light examined—whether as a gift, or an individual accumulation, or an exchange, or an inheritance—there is proof upon proof that there is a flaw in the rich man's title which takes away at once its very show of justice, and its value. The present wealth of the country was not given to the ancestors of these men some centuries since, for it did not then exist ; and if any could have been so given, it would long since have been consumed : it has not been acquired by successive accumulations of the produce of the labour of rich men, for, as a class, they have never been labourers ; and even if they had laboured, and laboured hard, they could not have amassed so much wealth : — it has not been obtained by equal exchanges, for, independent of a man's labour, equal exchanges will not make him rich :—it has not been acquired by inheritance—by the handing down of savings from one generation of working-men to another—for circumstances of every kind have been unfavourable to its transmission as well as to its accumulation :—but this wealth has all been derived from the bones and sinews of the working classes during successive ages, and it has been taken from them by the fraudulent and slavery-creating system of unequal exchanges.

The principle of unequal exchanges is the very life and soul of the present social system, and the inequality of every kind which is inseparable from it. Wherever this principle is acted upon, a man's riches, or his success in life, will be dependent neither upon his morality, nor his mental or corporeal faculties. Every individual has an undisputed right to the possession and enjoyment of any wealth which his industry or frugality will enable him to accumulate ; but let a working man under the present system, be as industrious and frugal as possible, the proceeds of his labour will never make him rich, nor enable him to live for any length of time without working. If he would become wealthy, he must change his position in society and instead of exchanging his *own labour*, must become a capitalist, or exchanger of *the labour of other people*; and thus, by plundering others in the same manner as he was plundered, through the medium of unequal exchanges, he will be enabled to acquire great gains from the small losses of other people.

The present system, wherever it enriches a working man, does it thus :—He has accumulated, or borrowed, we will suppose, £100, and takes his station as a capitalist ; he "speculates" with this money—that is, he makes an unjust and unequal exchange—he purchases a

commodity at one price, and without adding any increased
value to it by his own labour, he sells the commodity for
double the sum which it originally cost him : and thus he
becomes rich at the expense of others. Or again, he procures a certain quantity of labour for his hundred pounds,
and he sells the product of such labour for two hundred
pounds. Now, if the labour was originally worth two
hundred pounds, and this newly created capitalist gave
but one hundred for it, he has clearly defrauded his workmen of one-half their just due ; and if the labour was
worth only one hundred pounds, and the capitalist has
obtained two hundred for it, it is equally clear that he has
defrauded the parties with whom he made the second
exchange, for he only gave them the one hundred for their
two hundred.   All the gain thus acquired by the capitalist, whether from the first or the second exchange, is
extracted entirely from the productive classes.   Society at
large consists only of two parties—those who work, and
those who do nothing.   From the nature of the case, however, the idlers cannot have been defrauded by the
unequal exchange, for, as they do not labour, they can
have nothing of their own to exchange ; so that the whole
gain—the whole accumulated profit, or interest, or whatever
else it may be called, which every capitalist receives under
the present system—is taken from the producers at large
—from the very working class of the community, for they
only have wherewith to exchange—and that is, their
labour, and the produce of such labour.   The capitalist,
by thus continuing to " exchange," is shortly in possession
of as many thousands as he originally had hundreds—and
this, too, with little or no labour on his part—until at
length he retires to enjoy himself on his " honest gains."
The sons follow the course of the father—they live in
luxury and idleness, and so they become, and breed away,
ad infinitum, a race of " capitalists !"

Such is the origin of the great majority of petty capitalists who now grind the working classes into the dust.
But of all the vast wealth thus obtained by unequal
exchanges, it is self-evident that the original stock only—
the hundred pounds, or whatever it may be—is all that
each capitalist is justly entitled to.   This hundred pounds
belongs to the capitalist—it has, we will suppose, been the
produce of his own industry—and to it, therefore, he is

and the abasement of another. In connection with particular individuals and classes, however, Capital and Labour
can have no community of interest—they will ever be in
perpetual hostility—for the gain of the capitalist is always
the loss of the working man, and the poverty and toil of
the last is a necessary consequence of the wealth and the
idleness of the first.

Of all the vast wealth now existing in the United
Kingdom—worth, as it is, so many thousands of millions
sterling, and produced, as it has been, by the labour of
the productive classes during many centuries—of all this
immense wealth, the share which the working man holds
and enjoys is but as an ounce to a ton—a drop to an
ocean—in comparison to that which the present social
system has enabled the capitalists to obtain possession of.
The share of the working man has never yet been greater,
and never will be greater, even if millions upon millions
be annually produced, so long as the principle of unequal
exchanges is tolerated ; for this alone will maintain the
present division of society into capitalists and producers,
and rear the wealth and the supremacy of the one, upon
the poverty and the degradation of the other. When the
workman has produced a thing, it is his no longer—it
belongs to the capitalist—it has been conveyed from the
one to the other by the unseen magic of unequal exchanges.
The working man, notwithstanding all his toil, finding
himself as poor as ever, forthwith labours away to produce
more wealth ; and this, again, is conveyed to the capitalist in the same manner as the first was. And thus,
oppressed and plundered, must the working class toil on
to the end of the present social system ; for the capitalists
and the employers, as such, will always have interests
opposed to those of the producers at large. It is the
interest of the working man to acquire as much wealth as
posssible by means of his own labour—it is the interest of
the capitalist to acquire as much wealth as possible by
means of profit, or the labour of other people; and as all
profit must come from labour, and as the wealth of the
capitalist is but an accumulation of profit, the gain of the
capitalist must be the loss of the working man. The very
nature of the " exchange" which takes place between the
parties will inevitably perpetuate the wealth of the one
and the poverty of the other ; and thus effectually subvert

all equality of rights and laws, whatever may be the form
of government established, and whatever may be the merely
political power placed in the hands of the working man.

Under the present social system, the capitalists and
employers are not only distinct from, but they are in a
manner independent of, the working class. They have
the whole control of all the operations of trade—at their
fiat production goes forward, or languishes, or ceases altogether—the working man is made comparatively comfortable, or he starves by inches. In all trades and professions
the capitalist or employer receives double or quadruple
remuneration for single work, or for no work whatever.
This is the great source of Labour's wrongs. The essential principle of a well-constituted social system—EQUAL
EXCHANGES—is now unheeded, and the working men of
all trades are exposed to every wrong and every injustice
which the rapacity of their fellow-men can inflict upon
them. There is no social or governmental wrong which
is unconnected with the neglect of the great principle of
Equal Exchanges, or equal remuneration for equal labour;
so long as there is inequality of remuneration there must
be inequality of exchanges—there will be inequality
of wealth and condition—there will be evasion of
labour by some classes at the expense of other classes
—there will be rich and poor—there will be tyrants
and slaves. The whole question of remuneration and
exchanges resolves itself simply thus:—Shall fifty men
receive two pounds sterling each for a week's labour; or
shall they receive only one pound each, and give the
remaining fifty to the capitalist? The producers at large
can surely have but one opinion on this question; and
they will not for ever tolerate the glaring injustice which
gives to one man, for one man's labour, the same sum as is
given to fifty men for their whole united labour.

When the term " universal labour" is used, it is merely
meant to imply that all persons shall, at some period of
life, render society a proper equivalent for the benefits
which society has conferred upon them. This just principle has never yet been acted upon; for, one class has
conferred all benefits, and another class has received all.
Wealth will ever be created by the working class, and be
appropriated and enjoyed by the capitalists and proprietors, until equal exchanges shall compel the latter to

labour, and at the same time prevent them from obtaining possession of the fruits of the labour of others. The word "labour" applies not only to bodily and mental exertion in the business of direct production, but likewise to services of any kind which have a tendency to increase man's knowledge and happiness. We have faculties calculated for high as well as for low enjoyments; but the production and proper distribution of wealth is the first thing to be considered, because it forms the foundation on which the superstructure of pleasures essentially human must be based. The mind must be provided for as well as the body, or we fulfil but half the end of our existence, and enjoy but half the happiness of which that existence may be made susceptible. To this end there must always be division of labour—there will always be some whose mental superiority will qualify them to be the directors of their fellows—there will always be some who are pre-eminent in letters, and the arts and sciences—but all such are only parts of the great whole, and are as dependent on their fellows, as their fellows are upon them. As the dependence, therefore, is equal, the labour should be equal; and, whether the labour be equal or unequal, the remuneration should ever be in proportion to the labour, whatever may be the character or the results, or the end of that labour. Division of labour must never be lost sight of, for it is the lightener of man's toils, and the first step to civilization and refinement.

In defence of the present social system, the capitalists and employers, when they hear of dissatisfaction, tell us that the working class of the united kingdom have little or nothing to complain of—that they live under institutions comparatively free—that they can either work or let it alone—and that they are better fed, and clothed, and educated, than even kings were in times of old. To render yet more striking the contrast between the present and the past condition of the producers, old records are brought forth to show that the working men of former times were bought and sold, like so many horses, along with the estate to which they were attached—that their houses were but assemblages of sticks and stones, with windows destitute of glass—that they slept upon rushes strewed upon a damp clay floor, and had a log of wood for a pillow—that they lived upon the coarsest food, and scarcely tasted flesh a dozen times in the year—that they had neither books, newspapers, nor knowledge, and had to either work or fight as their masters and owners thought fit. If all this be true, and the working class be now much better off than their predecessors were, it is no reason why they should not be still better off, and equally as well off as those who tell them to hold their tongues, and be contented with the position which they now occupy. All happiness is comparative ; and it is not in human nature to remain satisfied with any station, so long as it is cognizant of a better ; nor will men submit to be measured by a low standard, so long as there is a higher one in existence. Why should enormous masses of wealth be in the possession of the idle and the profligate, when the industrious and the honest are without a penny ? Why should well-fed and well-clothed insignificance roll slothfully along in its splendid vehicle, in pursuit of new pleasures to tempt its palled appetite, and the toil-worn artizan be compelled to plod to his daily work, with half-clothed back and hungry belly ? There is no reason given, for there is not one to be found. The immaculate Spirit of Justice which exists throughout creation, tells men, in accents of eternal truth, that He never instituted these most unjust distinctions amongst them.

The productive classes of the United Kingdom are weighed to the earth by such a variety and multiplicity of burthens and wrongs, that enumeration and description both fail in bringing into view the sum total. The ills they suffer are brought home to them through every sense ; for sight, hearing, smell, taste, and feeling alike proclaim the wrong, and tell men that a remedy is needed. These evils are so interwoven into the present system—so ramified and entangled—so assimilated into every social and political institution—that the productive class can only free themselves by cutting through all at one blow. Every mere governmental remedy has been proved fallacious and useless. One remedy yet remains to be tried, and one only—that of changing the very course of human society, and sweeping away, at once, the accumulated wrongs of thousands of years. Some amongst us may start at the magnitude of the remedy proposed, but the change is no more than will be necessary to effect the gigantic evil which consumes us. Let those who think that less will do, turn over the page of history—let them look back to the working man of all ages, under all forms of government, under all systems of religion—and they will find that the wrongs and the evils of which we now complain have always existed. Has not every effort, petty or mighty, moral or physical, been insufficient to shake off that crushing incubus which has for so many ages deadened the soul of the producer of wealth ? Does not every struggle of the working man fail to subvert that unseen power which chains his prostrated energies to the ever-moving oar of capital, and gives him up, bound body and soul, to every ill that the governmental and ecclesiastical tyranny of class and caste may choose to inflict upon him ? If despotism, or the exercise of undelegated authority by particular individuals and classes, could have done it, there has been despotism enough — if liberty, either as merging into licentiousness, or as connected with obedience to a political authority self-imposed and subject to popular control, could have done it, there has at times been liberty enough—if prayers, and sacrifices, and burnt-offerings could have done it, the shouting and the incense-smoke which have ascended upwards for four thousand years would have prevailed ! Away, then, with any and every remedy which falls short of the establishment of First Principles. This is the only remedy which man has not yet tried ; and from the nature of the wrong, it is the only remedy which can be effective.

CHAPTER V.

THE GOVERNMENTAL BURTHENS OF THE WORKING
CLASS OF THE UNITED KINGDOM.

IN that interminable torrent of progression in which all
things move man may make attempts to stand still, but
all his efforts will be futile. What he considers perfect
to-day, he is willing to alter a little to-morrow. The
omnipresent spirit of Motion is within him and around
him ; and, almost without being conscious of it, man
moves along with the rest of things. Although thus perpetually changing and making changes, men scarcely ever
like these changes when subjected to their influence for
the first time. We become accustomed to go through
life, as it were, in a kind of jog-trot ; and anything which
tends to accelerate our speed, or make our journey more
easy and pleasant, is always, at the beginning regarded
with dislike. Afterwards, however, when we have become
habituated to the new order of things, and are about to
make a further remove, we cling to the last change with as
much pertinacity as we at first displayed in rejecting it.
Although old shoes may fit us easier than new ones, we
are never thereby prevented from throwing the old aside
and obtaining the new; for everything—an institution as
well as an article of apparel—must be new before it can
be old.

Men have in all ages cried out against changes of every
description ; and if their dolorous prognostications of the
evils attendant on changes could have retarded the march
of events, we should now have been no better than naked
and half-famished savages ; for the barbarian, like the
civilised man, has the best possible social system, the best
form of government, and the most rational religious belief,
that man can institute or the Creator of man ordain.

Since, then, we have progressed thus far, why should we not take another leap, and make the world all that poets ever dreamed of, or good men ever longed for? Why should we not institute a system of action, with regard to each other, based on those immutable principles of justice and equality which alone are capable of making man as happy as he is mighty? We have seen plainly that, by the present constitution of society, the millions are a doomed class—that, from the position in which they stand with regard to capital and the capitalist, their condition is unimprovable and their wrongs irremediable—and that, as a body, they will remain oppressed and impoverished, even if they produce a million of pounds sterling worth of wealth in the place of every thousand which they now create. The subversion of this unjust system, and the institution of one more in accordance with the nature and attributes of man, will be anything but difficult ; and we should be bound to attempt the change, if success were only just within the verge of possibility.

If the productive classes require a stimulus to exertion in the noble cause of their redemption, let them view, side by side, their governmental and their social burthens— those attributable to monarchy, and those arising from that system of inequality of which monarchy is no more than the impersonation—and it will be seen that the working classes of the United Kingdom are, by unequal exchanges, annually plundered of the produce of their labour to an amount almost incalculable ; and that, so long as this system of unequal exchanges is tolerated, the producers will be almost as poor and as ignorant and as hard-worked as they are at present, even if *every* governmental burthen be swept away, and all taxes be abolished.

The mere fact that our present social system enables hundreds of thousands of able-bodied men to exist in uselessness, and without returning any equivalent for the many benefits which they receive, ought to be a sufficient proof to every producer, that the system is a bad one. The gain of an idle class must necessarily be the loss of an industrious class : and although the manner in which the former obtain possession of their wealth may be called legal, yet is the transaction nothing less than a robbery upon the working man. It is these idlers only who deny that the producers are plundered. These capitalists and proprietors do not attempt to assert that they live without eating and drinking, but they gravely affirm that they have a just claim upon the workman for subsistence—that they have a perfect right to enjoy life without labour. They found their claims upon their own assertions, that the land belongs to them, the houses belong to them— the machinery and money belong to them—everything belongs to them. They tell us, moreover, that there is perfect reciprocity of benefits between the capitalist and the working man ; and that the former is justly entitled to a share of the produce of the latter, in consideration of allow- ing him to make use of those accumulations which the present system enables the capitalist to obtain possession of.

We have already seen that these capitalists and proprie- tors never had, and never can have as individuals, any right to the exclusive possession of either the land or the accumulations ;—that the land was never given especially to them by the Creator, nor sold to them by him, nor given to other parties who had power to sell it, or give it, but that it is a gift to all living beings in common ; and that the accumulations now in existence have been pro- duced by Labour, and to Labour only, therefore, do they justly belong, for no equivalent has the capitalist yet given for them. But even if all the land and the machi- nery and the houses did belong to the capitalists, and the working class were not in being, the former would not there- by be enabled to evade the great condition "that there shall be labour." Their wealth would leave them the choice only of working or starving. They cannot eat the land and the houses; and the land will not yield sustenance, nor the machinery make clothing. without the application of human labour. Therefore, when the capitalists and proprietors say that the working class must support them, they likewise say, in effect, that the producers belong to them as well as the houses and lands do—that the working man was created only for the rich man's use ! If particular classes have received a special license from the Almighty, to have and to hold all that is good on earth, and to keep the labourer in eternal bondage, let them shew the record, and we will speak no more of the wrongs of the working class.

Every working man of the United Kingdom knows and feels that he is a member of a plundered and degraded and despised class, but he is ignorant of one half of the burthens which he sustains. The greater part of his load is unseen by him, and it is this circumstance which causes him to bear his lot so long and so unrepiningly. Their governmental burthens—their enormous taxes—are believed, by most of his order, to be all that they sustain ; and to get rid of these, they would have a share in the government, through the instrumentality of universal suffrage—or they would alter the very form of their government, and exchange an irresponsible king or queen for a chief magistrate elected by themselves. When, however, the working class have viewed their social as well as their governmental wrongs—when they have compared the drain of the one with the drain of the other—when they become conscious of the immense amount of wealth which the present system enables certain classes of the community to abstract from them—they will scout the idea of any change which falls short of the total subversion of this system and the establishment of one founded on the broad principles of justice and equality which we have been considering.

Man has ever yet been the property of man ; and no mere governmental change, if engrafted upon the present social system, will permit him to be otherwise. Although we have long thrown away the name and the livery of slavery, yet are the working classes no less owned than their ancestors were in times of old. They toil, while others are idle—they produce, and others consume—the one class order, and the other obey—therefore are the producers still slaves, in the true sense of the term ; and alike suffering as they suffer, and toiling as they toil, are the enslaved millions of king-governed Europe, and the shadow-grasping millions of republican America. Whatever else may be done, the principle and practice of slavery can never be destroyed, nor can man become truly free, until labour be universal and exchanges equal.

There are in the present year A.D. 1838, in the United Kingdom of Great Britain and Ireland, about 25,000,000 of inhabitants,—men, women, and children. To support the general government of the country, pay the interest of what is called the "National Debt," and the numberless pensions and salaries enjoyed by those who rule us, there is raised and expended annually about £50,000,000. Of this vast sum—greater, perhaps, than is received by any other government in existence—nearly £28,000,000 is required for the "interest" of the National Debt—about £7,000,000 is taken for the support of an army of 100,000 men—£5,000,000 is wanted for the navy and ordnance—and the remainder is swallowed up in pensions, salaries, and other expenses connected with that complicated machine called monarchical government. To the £50,000,000 squandered in this manner, by the general government, must be added the many rates annually raised for the support of the local governments connected with counties, towns, and parishes, and which likewise amount to many millions sterling.

The "National Debt"—the interest of which forms so prominent a feature in our expenditure—formerly amounted to above one thousand millions of pounds sterling; but is now rather under eight hundred millions. This enormous sum was partly borrowed, and partly pretended to be borrowed, from certain persons in our own country, by an irresponsible and tyrannical government, for the purpose of carrying on bloody and exterminating wars against almost every nation on the face of the earth. The future will in vain ask of the past what benefits resulted from these wars; but the debt contracted on their account, although pretended to be still in existence, has been paid by the productive classes two or three times over, through the medium of what goes by the name of "interest," and by changes in the currency.

	£.
In 1688 this debt was	664,263
In 1702	16,394,702
In 1714	54,145,363
In 1775	128,583,635
In 1793	239,350,148
At the Peace, in 1815	1,050,000,000

We often hear of the gross ignorance and brutality of the people of former ages, and of the spread of true religion in modern times. A bloated and self-appointed hierarchy weekly proclaim the moral revolution effected at home and abroad by hosts of priests and missionaries, and daily reiterate their calls for contributions to carry forward the holy work. But the progress of this national debt, gives the lie direct

to all these boasted ecclesiastical performances; and pro-
claims, in a voice which pulpit declamation cannot drown,
that, however creeds and dogmas may change to suit the
spirit of the times, true religion is as much unknown in the
present century as it was in the fire-and-faggot times of
Popish persecution. This debt, and the wholesale massacres
connected with it, have steadily kept pace with modern
art, and science, and religion; and every engine of
destruction which ingenuity could invent, has been
employed by modern Christian rulers and defenders of the
church, in the ancient kingly pastime of extermination.
All history tells alike the same tale of kingcraft and priestcraft; with which, and the present social system, true religion can have nothing to do.

The £800,000,000 to which the debt has been reduced,
is said to be owing, by the nation at large, to about 279,751
individuals in various ranks of society, and these persons
receive the annual £28,000,000 of interest amongst them,
for which they render no labour whatever.

The immense increase which has taken place in this debt
in later times, was occasioned,—not by endeavours to repel
aggressions from bands of ruthless invaders—not by exertions in the cause of civilisation and refinement—not by
efforts to conquer the powers of nature, and make them
subservient to the happiness of man—but by the insane
attempts of a despotic and ignorant British government to
arrest the march of mind, and keep down the soul of man,
and the rising spirit of liberty. This government, however, desperately wicked and brutally depraved as it was,
arose spontaneously from our present social system—our
system of classes with opposing interests: the atrocious
acts perpetrated by this government resulted from its very
constitution—from the habits, opinions, and position in
society of the men composing it; and such detestable
crimes, and the like profligate waste of money, have always
resulted and ever will invariably result from every government
so constituted—from every government arising from a part
instead of a whole—from every government formed of and
by rich men.

The truth of this assertion is not disproved by the present condition of the people of the United States, whose
government has not yet committed such crimes against
whole nations—who owe no debt—and who call themselves

Republicans. Their position, and their poverty in regard to men and money, have so far saved them. But it has already been shewn, that from the very nature of things there can never be a true republic—there can never be equal rights and equal laws—under the present social system. This system itself—whatever may be the form of government instituted at any particular time—has an invariable and inevitable tendency to generate inequality of wealth, and therefore every other description of inequality ; and must sooner or later merge all republics into monarchies, or despotisms of some kind ,as all history proves to us. The same mighty principle of evil—inequality of wealth in connection with the gradation of classes—has pervaded almost every nation and every form of government which has existed ; and the same wrongs and miseries have ultimately befallen the working class under republics as under monarchies. The United States' government, whatever it may be called, is, like that of Britain, the government of a class—the government of the men of money ; and there is no flagrant violation of justice—no wanton outrage upon the rights of man—which that government does not permit to be openly practised, by its half-hatched aristocracy, upon the two millions of enslaved human beings in the republic ; nor does any European war of aggression—any effort of a crowned despot to establish man's supremacy over man—offer one feature of injustice or outrage which is not likewise to be beheld in the United States' war of usurpation and extermination against the aboriginal inhabitants of that portion of America.

In addition to the vast sums which have been wrung from the people of the United Kingdom, and wasted for such abominable purposes as the destruction of human life and the enslavement of body and mind, we must take into account the blood spilled, the tears shed, the hearts broken, throughout the enacting of the long and dire tragedy. These form the blackest and the heaviest items in the account of monarchical misrule. During the last century or two, there have been twenty-four wars between England and France, twelve between England and Scotland, eight between England and Spain, and seven between England and other nations—in all, fifty-one ! The ascertained amount of British money expended, during the last six great wars, is as follows :—

		£
1. War ending 1697, cost	......	21,500,000
2. War ending 1712, cost	......	43,000,000
3. War ending 1737, cost	......	46,000,000
4. War ending 1756, cost	......	111,000,000
5. American War, 1775, cost	....	139,000,000
6. War from 1793 to 1815 cost	..	850,000,000

These sums, doubtless, fall far short of the actual amount expended ; for the real cost of war is unknown and unappreciable. Besides the money thus sacrificed, the number of human beings that perished during four of these wars have been thus estimated :—

War ending 1697	{ 100,000 slain.
	{ 80,000 died of famine.
War ending 1756........	250,000 slain.
War of 1775............	200,000 slain.
War from 1793 to 1815,.2,000,000 slain !	

But these wars have cost other nations much, as well as the people of the United Kingdom. The very last long war, from 1793 to 1815, besides burthening Britain to the amount of £850,000,000, cost :—

	£
France	690,000,000
Austria.........................	220,000,000
The other Sates of Europe 1,012,000,000	
The United States of America	27,000,000

Forming a total of £2,699,000,000—all wasted—all worse than wasted—by men calling themselves Christians, for the purpose of plundering and destroying other Christians! These vast numbers slain, and this immense amount of money lost, includes only the fighting men, and the sums spent by the several governments engaged. The more innocent victims of the demoniac spirit of inequality—the fathers, and mothers, and children, amongst the people of the several countries, who perished by violence, and the misery and want inseparable from war—are not placed in the account. Their ruined homes, and plundered wealth, and blighted happiness, count as nothing in the cost, when despotism estimates its losses !

Although most of these wars and crimes and losses may

be ascribed to the existence of the monarchical form of government, with its irresponsibility and its "right divine," it must never be forgotten, when we enumerate our wrongs and look for remedies, that the monarchical form is the natural and spontaneous production of the present social system; and that, therefore, this form can never be permanently altered, nor the miseries and wrongs which flow from it be escaped from, unless the parent and the cause—the system—be itself changed. Were all Europe to be revolutionised and republicanised to-morrow, and an absolute equality of mere governmental power to be established amongst the people of the several States, such equality would totally disappear before the end of twenty years. Society at large is thoroughly imbued with the rampant spirit of inequality and exclusiveness—inequality and exclusiveness in respect to worldly condition, and education, and caste—and this inequality and exclusiveness would speedily generate institutions agreeable to their own nature, and destructive of any political equality which might be established. History gives us ten thousand damning proofs of the inherent corruption of the system of inequality, in the ultimate subversion of all just governmental institutions.

The capitalists and economists tell us that the enormous taxes required to support our government fall alike upon all classes of the community—upon the wealthy idler as well as upon the industrious producer—and that, in fact, the rich capitalist pays a much greater amount than the working man. If we looked only at the taxes paid by each class directly—without taking into consideration where these taxes come from, and who are the persons that bring them into existence—it certainly would appear as if the greater weight fell upon the rich man; but it is not in this way that the working man must estimate his burthen. We have only to regard the first great condition of production—the creator of all wealth and the supporter of all taxation—"That there shall be labour,"—and we see at once that, so far from the capitalists and proprietors paying the greatest amount of taxes, they in reality *pay nothing whatever !* We discover that the productive classes, and the productive classes only, pay the whole amount. If a man assist not in production, he can have nothing *of his own* wherewith to pay taxes; and therefore, although the mere capitalists and wealthy proprietors may pay certain sums to the tax-gatherer, they pay them only nominally. The money thus paid merely passes through their hands ; for, as they are non-producers, it could never justly belong to them ; and therefore it is a complete perversion of language—a gross falsity—to say that these men pay taxes, when they have neither produced them, nor given any equivalent for them.

Under the present social system, the capitalist is placed in such a position, that no tax whatever, whether great or small, direct or indirect, can touch *him*. He is out of the reach of taxation ; and he is so because he is beyond the pale of production. While he continues to be a non-producer, no property or income tax can gain anything from him. Such modes of taxation would merely compel the capitalist to disgorge a part of the wealth which unequal exchanges had enabled him to obtain from the working man. The relief which the latter would obtain by such disgorging, and by such a plan of raising taxes, would, however, be only apparent ; for the very position of the capitalist, as the exclusive holder of the soil, as exclusive possessor of the national accumulations, and as the exclusive controller of the labour of the people, enables him, by raising profits or lowering wages, to reimburse himself for any loss which he may sustain by means of taxation. An income or property tax would never actually make the class of capitalists one penny poorer, nor the working class one penny richer, than they are at the present moment. The rich would still maintain their wealth and their supremacy, and flourish, as they now do, upon the wrongs of the working man. We never had, and never can have, any possible method of coming at the capitalist, and uprooting the poison tree of his unhallowed dominion, but that of establishing the great laws of UNIVERSAL LABOUR and EQUAL EXCHANGES. This is the only brand which can stay their hydra-headed growth for ever !

Thus, when we go to the origin of the wealth of the capitalist, and unmask the transaction which takes place between him and the working man, it is most palpably apparent that the whole enormous taxation of the United Kingdom—the fifty millions of pounds sterling consumed by the general government, as well as the many millions levied in rates for the support of the various local governments—rests solely upon the productive classes !—upon those classes of which the working man is the foundation and the supporter !   All the lavish expenditure and profligate and shameless waste which has ever characterised the British Government beyond that of any other on the face of the earth, comes at once from the pockets of the productive classes—has been produced through the instrumentality of their heads, and bones, and sinews; and yet they are told that they are not plundered—that the burthen of taxation rests not upon them !   The producer once believed that this gross falsehood was the truth—he was once ignorant that the labour of his class created all wealth—and he foolishly thought that the taxes which the capitalist appeared to give up, were paid by him in reality. But the darkness of ignorance has passed away from before the working man—he has found out how it comes to pass that some men are rich and some poor, some men employers and some employed—he has discovered how unequal exchanges make the gain of the first to be the loss of the last ;—and he now sees, by the full glare of Reason's day-light, that all wealth comes from him—that all taxes are paid by him—that all the idleness and pomp and vainglory which oppresses and insults and defies him, is maintained in its power and efficiency at his cost !

Here, then, is an answer to those who say that the productive classes are not plundered.   Here is a sum of fifty millions sterling which the enemies of Labour acknowledge that they yearly receive for the support of what they call a " government ;" and it has been proved, upon principles which cannot be controverted, that not one farthing of this money comes from the non-productive capitalist and proprietor.   Here is nearly one-sixth of the annual value of the labour of a great nation swallowed up by its government !   Here is £50,000,000 annually taken by this government, that the industrious people may be protected from robbery !—hundreds of thousands of them slain, that they may live in peace and harmony !—every law of nature and of justice outraged, that they may learn religion and morality !

Well might thousands and hundreds of thousands of the productive classes of the United Kingdom look, for relief, to an alteration in the form of their government—well might they view, with envy, the economical system of the United States, and sigh for a republic ;—and to a revolution, and the establishment of a similar republic in the United Kingdom, the long-endured oppression and increasing misery of the working classes must soon inevitably lead us, had we not another and a better end in view. A change in the form of the British Government—a change from a hereditary and irresponsible dynasty to that elective and representative form called a republic—would apparently save the productive classes a few millions sterling per annum; but they have a far mightier object within their grasp than the accomplishment of a simple governmental change; for experience has taught them that, under the existing social system, no form of government can long remain effective of good to the people.

It is now, then, no longer a question between the governed and the governors—no longer an affair merely of pounds, shillings, and pence; but the present is a matter between man and man—it is a question of justice or injustice, of equality or inequality, of exaltation or degradation—it is, to the working man, a question of life or death ! A movement amongst the masses of the United Kingdom will inevitably take place—upon the objects of that movement will depend its success as a means, and its value as an end. The subversion of a social system, it will be shewn, when determined upon by a people, is as easy a matter as the subversion of a government ;—and, having the true wrong and the true remedy before them, the productive classes surely will not, by attempting to obtain a part rather than the whole, re-fasten the chains which are falling from them, nor endure in perpetuity the accumulated ills and wrongs which their class have sustained since the commencement of civilization. With less than a social change, the blood and the tears of the toil-worn will be for ever drunk up, with a searing and consuming fire, from the golden altars of " CAPITAL." There will on the side of the last be no remorse—there can for the miseries of the first be no relief.

It is the common practice of the self-styled wise men of all generations, to declaim against any changes which are above their own shallow comprehension, or which extend beyond the contracted circle of themselves and their class. Such persons appear to have no idea that the world can go, in after times, any way different to what it went at the precise time they existed. The past is a blank to them, and therefore the future is as a sealed book. To such men, everything that happens to be farther from their eyes than the ends of their own noses, is "visionary"—everything which they will not set themselves to perform, is unaccomplishable by others. There are many of these mental blinkards at the present day ; and any man who dares but to hope that the sons of labour shall not always be oppressed and enslaved—that men will not always be compelled, by circumstances, to hate and injure each other—that wars shall cease, and mankind dwell together in harmony,—any man who dares thus to hope that a brighter and a better day is coming, is the most visionary of all visionaries ! The terms love, and charity, and morality, imply—if interpreted by the acts of these wide-mouthed and narrow-ribbed screamers against innovation—not things to be felt, and practised, and enjoyed, but certain effete and incomprehensible essences, to be preached about in pulpit and platform harangues for the edification of the poor and the oppressed.

Generated by the present system, and fattening on its corruptions, we never find these scorners of good men and good works to be in poverty—we never find them honourably and laboriously engaged in the production of wealth—but, like the scum upon the boiling pot, they dance upon the surface of society—they are ever well to do in the world—always on the watch for " profit." The vocation of such men is, to buy cheap and sell dear—to accumulate wealth by unjust and unequal exchanges—to batten upon the fruits of the workman's toil. These drivellers loudly inculcate the practice of morality and virtue ; but, although they see vice and misery overspreading the whole earth, and every moral injunction unheeded and unfulfilled,—these self-justified Pharisees will themselves do nothing towards accomplishing the end which they so often profess to have in view. On the contrary, they are perpetually spouting forth their frothy and unmeaning gabble against all innovators and all changes. The world must wait their bidding to move forward, or they hiss and scream like frightened geese.

The injunctions and precepts of religion and morality are intended as rules for human guidance, or they are not : if they be not so intended, and are no more than the distempered ravings of some enthusiastic visionary, we can at any time lay them aside ; but if they are intended to be fulfilled and abided by, and we find that our present social system utterly precludes such fulfilment, then are men bound to alter this system, and to institute such social arrangements as will enable them to carry out, to the fullest extent, those important principles. Let those who uphold the present system shew, if they can, that it is impossible for human beings to dwell together more har-moniously than they do at present—that there will continue to be the same incentives to vice and ill-will as there now are, if men establish a system which will guarantee equal rights, by enforcing equal duties. We can show those who will not hear of social changes—all history will prove to them—that the social institutions of man have hitherto been incompatible with the existence of equal rights, or charity, or morality, or true unity ; and if these things are necessary to our happiness, then must we, as rational beings, eschew all institutions and modes of action that are subversive of so many things essential to human hap-piness.

CHAPTER VI.

THE SOCIAL BURTHENS OF THE WORKING CLASS OF THE UNITED KINGDOM.

A CONSIDERATION of the nature of wealth, and of the conditions necessary to its creation, has shewn us that the whole accumulated taxation of the empire rests entirely upon the productive classes ; that it is thus made to rest upon them through the instrumentality of the present system of unequal exchanges; and a further consideration will prove the truth of the assertion which has been made, that this taxation, great as it is confessed to be, sinks into insignificance when compared with the other pecuniary burthens which the present social system compels the productive classes to sustain.

We will now, then, bring into view, and place in the account of their losses, that indirect and almost unseen transfer of wealth from the working class to the capitalist, which is hourly taking place through the instrumentality of that same accursed system of unequal exchanges which makes the former bear all the governmental burthens. We have no correct returns for this part of Labour's outgoings. The account would be too startling, too astounding, too destructive of every civil institution now existing, to be given by any government arising from, and existing in connection with, the present social system. Although it may not be possible to ascertain precisely the sum which is thus abstracted from the working classes, we may approximate sufficiently near the truth to form a just conception of the magnitude of the wrongs inflicted upon them ; and we shall at the same time perceive, more clearly, the utter fatuity of expecting permanent relief from any change short of an entire change of system.

As a first step to the calculation, we will suppose the population of the United Kingdom of Great Britain and Ireland to be, in round numbers, 25,000,000 of human beings. All these individuals must be fed, clothed, and housed in some way or other—they all make a perpetual call upon the material of subsistence, whether they labour or not, and whether much or little is produced by those who perform the labour. Some of them, perhaps, consume and waste their thousands of pounds sterling a year, whilst others starve upon as many thousand pennies. But if we take every thing into consideration—the comparative numbers of rich and poor, the price of food and clothing, and the number of children—we may safely, for the sake of data, estimate the entire maintenance of the twenty-five millions of people to be worth, on the average, at least £15 per head annually. This gives £375,000,000 as the yearly value of the maintenance of the whole people of the United Kingdom. We do not, however, employ ourselves merely in producing articles of subsistence, for our labour creates, likewise, many unconsumable articles. We every year add to our stock of accumulations, or capital, by increasing the number of our houses, ships, implements, machines, roads, and other assistants to further production, besides making good all wear and tear. Thus, although our subsistence may be worth but three hundred and seventy-five millions sterling a year, the total annual value of the wealth created by the people of the United Kingdom will not be less than five hundred millions sterling. A near approximation to this result has been given at various times, and by different persons; and, in the present state of statistics, it is perhaps as near the truth as we can arrive.

This vast amount of wealth, let it be borne in mind, is not created by the labour of every individual comprised in the twenty-five millions of inhabitants. The half of this number are females; and of the remaining half, some are too old to work, some too young, some too lazy, and some cannot get work to do; so that we cannot calculate upon having above one-fourth of our population, or about six millions of men—that is, those between the ages of fourteen and fifty—as effective producers. Of this number, however, scarcely five millions can be said, under the present arrangements of society, to assist in production;

for thousands of able-bodied men in Great Britain are compelled to stand idle while the work which they ought to do is being performed by women and children ; and hundreds of thousands of men in Ireland can obtain no employment whatever.   Thus less than five millions of men, assisted by a few thousands of women and children, have not only to create produce for the consumption of themselves and families, but likewise for the whole mass of willing and unwilling idlers, and unprofitable labourers of every description, amounting in the aggregate to twenty-five millions of human beings.

If we were without the vast accumulations of machinery of various kinds which we possess, society would not be in the state in which it now is.   There would neither be so many rich nor so many poor : for the present number of working men, if unassisted by machinery, could not support themselves and the present number of idlers and unprofitable labourers in the manner in which all are now supported.   The agricultural and manufacturing machinery of every kind which we bring to our aid in the business of production, has been computed to perform the labour of about one hundred millions of effective men.   It is this giant auxiliary that has assisted us to repair the vast losses which we have suffered by the wasteful and almost incessant wars in which we have been engaged : it is this mighty power which enables the productive classes of Britain to create an amount of wealth adequate to support the enormous drain which is perpetually taking place upon them : it is this gigantic instrument of good or evil —this machinery—and its application under the present system, which has generated the hundreds of thousands of idlers and livers on profit who now press the working class into the earth.

Thus machinery contains within itself both a bane and an antidote ; for while it has, more than any other thing, been a means of bringing about the present social crisis, it has at the same time opened a path by which every endured and every threatened evil may be escaped from. The present constitution of society has been fertilized by machinery, and by machinery will it be destroyed.   The steam-engine, although it creates wealth, has nothing to do with the application or appropriation of it ; and whatever may be the inequality of condition and the suffering

generated by the operation of this great power, the power
itself is not accountable for such things, and its destruction would not be the true remedy.   The machinery itself
is good—is indispensable ; it is the application of it—the
circumstance of its being possessed by individuals instead
of by the nation—that is bad.   So long as machinery is
thus exclusively possessed by individuals and classes, its
advantages will be partially enjoyed—it will be a curse
rather than a blessing to those classes of the community
by whom it is not possessed ; for it dooms them to be the
slaves and the prey of their fellows.

It is the great object of man, in all states of society, to
obtain the greatest possible amount of enjoyment with the
least possible pain and labour to himself ; and everything
which helps him to attain this end, must of itself be good.
Of all the assistants, however, which human ingenuity has
yet called into existence, none are so important as those
contrivances which compel fire and water, and wood and
iron, to do the work of human bones and muscles.   The
present poverty of the working class arises, not from the
fact that their labour is superseded by machinery, but
from the circumstance that nearly the whole of the wealth
created by the machinery is swallowed up by the rapa-
cious aristocracy of the hall parlour and the mill counting-
house.

The five millions of men already enumerated as assisting
in production, will include all who labour little or much—
the actual distributors as well as the producers—all those
who can be said to yield society any equivalent for the
benefits they receive.   Some of these persons do not work
five hours a day, while others, again, toil on for fifteen
hours ; and when to this is added the time lost by the
compulsory idleness of great numbers in times of depression in trade, it will be found that our annual production
is created and distributed by less than one-fifth of the
community, working, on the average, ten hours a day.

Thus it appears that there are nearly one million of
able-bodied men who do nothing towards the production or
proper distribution of wealth,—comprising landed proprietors, large capitalists, soldiers, &c.   But if we suppose
that the wealthy non-producers of every description, with
their families, and dependents, amount only to two millions of persons, yet this number alone would cost the

working classes £30,000,000 annually, if their maintenance were averaged, like that of the latter, at £15 per
head.   But it so happens, that the great body of these
non-producers belong to what is termed the " independent"
order—that they waste, or consume unprofitably, a great
part of the conveniences and nearly all the luxuries which
the toils of the working classes produce ; therefore, upon
the most moderate computation their maintenance will
cost not less than £50 per head.   This gives a total of
£100,000,000 as the annual cost of the mere drones of
society—the utterly unproductive, and worthless, either
in respect to ornament or use !

It is in this manner, and on this principle, that the
working classes must estimate their burthens.   Here it
is at once seen, that the mere idlers of the community
annually absorb an amount of wealth, above double that of
the whole governmental taxation of the empire !   And the
common sense of every man will at once tell him, that,
under the present arrangements of society, no change of
government—no political power possessed by the working
class—could save them *this* sum.   It would be taken from
them just the same under an economical republic as it is
under a profligate monarchy.

It has been laid down as a principle, recommended by
reason and sanctioned by justice, that all those who perform equal labour should receive an equal reward.   It is
only by acting upon this principle that the present order
of things can be done away with, and equality of rights
be established and enjoyed.   Under present arrangements,
however, the reward is greatest where the labour is least ;
and of the five millions of men engaged in production and
distribution in the United Kingdom, the remuneration is
as unequally and as unjustly bestowed as it is possible for
it to be.   Thus, in estimating their losses under the present
system, the working class must put into the account,—
not only the whole expense of the general and local government, amounting to at least the annual sum of £60,000,000
—not only the cost of the wealthy drones, and idlers. and
unproductive labourers, amounting to the annual sum of
£100,000,000—but likewise the double and quadruple
allowance received by the various classes of small proprietors, manufacturers, and tradesmen, in the shape of profit
and interest.   Upon the most moderate computation, the

share of wealth enjoyed by this extensive portion of the community will amount to not less than £140,000,000 annually, *above the average of what is received by an equal number of the best paid of the working class.* Thus, along with *their* government, the two classes of idlers and livers on profit—comprising, perhaps, one-fourth of the entire population—absorb about £300,000,000 annually, or above one-half of the entire wealth produced! *This* is the great wrong —*this* is the evil for which the working classes want a remedy—*this* is the secret enemy that devours them.

In the various sums and numbers here mentioned, none are supposed to be precisely correct, for we have few data, except those furnished by observation and experience, from which calculations can be made. As a whole, they may be greater or less; but, as parts, they will bear about the same mutual relation as is here assigned them. They are but examples of the working of the present system of unequal exchanges, and shew the utter inutility of simple governmental changes in alleviating burthens inseparably connected with the social system. The present arrangements of society, therefore, it is plainly seen, cost the working classes, in taxes to government and in rent and profit to proprietors and capitalists, the enormous annual sum of £300,000,000 sterling, which is an average loss of above £50 per head to every working man in the empire!—This leaves no more than an average of about £11 per head per annum, to be divided amongst the remaining three-fourths of the nation. From calculations made in 1815, it appears that the annual income of the whole people of the United Kingdom amounted to about £430,000,000 ; of which the working class received £99,742,547, and the rent, pension, and profit class £330,778,825 ! The whole property in the country was at the same time calculated to be worth nearly three thousand millions of pounds sterling.

There is, perhaps, scarcely one man in the United Kingdom who is ignorant of the fact, that there are many hundred idlers in the country who receive £10,000 or £20,000 a year in what are called rents and profits. For these sums, no equivalent is rendered to society at large; but this money is exacted by sundry proprietors, because certain persons occupy houses or grow corn upon lands which these non-producers tell us belong to *them.* We have al-

ready seen, from a consideration of the conditions connected
with these possessions, that the capitalists and proprietors,
as such, have no claim to them—that they never produced
either the lands or the houses, nor gave any real equivalent for them—but that these possessions truly and justly
belong to the nation as a whole. Notwithstanding, however, the gross wrong committed upon the productive
classes, the capitalists and proprietors have hitherto received
this money almost unquestioned. But it has been perceived by them, that the present fraudulent system could
not always go on unexamined—that the insufferable burthens sustained by the working class would be certain,
sooner, or later, to incite them to inquire what became of
the vast amount of wealth annually drawn from them—
and that they would set about devising remedies. The
capitalist, therefore, and the livers on rent and profit—
ever ready to excuse their rapacity, and maintain themselves in wealth and idleness at the expense of the working
class—have endeavoured to render to the latter an account
of their stewardship, that the plundered might not trouble
themselves by inquiring into the subject. To this end,
they tell us that it is utterly impossible for any individual
to consume £10,000 or £20,000 a year; and that of the
sum so received by any idler, a very small portion only is
consumed by himself and family—the remainder being
employed in setting labour in motion, and thus assisting
in further production; so that, in reality, the rich and idle
capitalist and proprietor are of great benefit to society,
because they fulfil the duties of distributors! Thus, the
advocates for exorbitant individual wealth and inequality
of condition endeavour to make it appear, that the actual
loss to the working part of the community, by these rich
idlers, is only just so much as the individuals themselves
consume—not the whole of £20,000 which they yearly
receive and spend. Admitting this to be the case, the loss
to the working class will still amount annually to the
£100,000,000 before stated; for the loss is occasioned by
the unprofitable employment and the waste of labour
which these idlers cause, as well as by their mere maintenance. The man of £20,000 a year will keep his servants,
horses, dogs, and other incumbrances, none of which—
although all of them may work—yield any actual service
to the community at large: they are not engaged in the

business of production, nor are they advancing, in any way, the interests of society : they give no profitable la_bour in exchange for the maintenance they receive ; and therefore their consumption, as well as that of their em_ployer, the idler, is a dead loss to the producing community.

There are many, even amongst the working class, who still think, as they have been taught to think, that these " independent" idlers are a great blessing to the commu_nity. " Look," cry these benighted men, " how Lord So_and-so spends his money ! See what numbers of servants, and horses, and dogs he keeps, and how good it makes trade ! Were it not for such as him, poor folks like us would starve !" It is sickening and pitiable to hear such exclamations as these come from the very same despised and oppressed beings from whom the money was originally taken !—who thus manifest an almost idiotic joy at behold_ing a wholesale plunderer squander away *their* money !— money produced by *their* toil and deprivation !

It is well that we are no longer ignorant that Labour is the creator of all wealth, or we might suppose that the vast sums annually received by capitalists and landed pro_prietors were paid by their tenants, because the money comes directly from them. But these tenants do not in reality pay the rent, for they lay the whole of it upon their produce. The consumers of the produce then ap_pear to pay it ; but all those consumers who belong to the trading classes cover themselves by placing a certain profit upon the articles in which they deal. Thus the charge is perpetually shifted from one class to the class immediately below it, until, at length, its whole accumulated weight rests solely upon the working class. Without labour there can be no production—no rent—and the rent or profit receiv_ed by any proprietor or capitalist, is but the representative of so much produce and so much labour.

As it has been before observed, the present system of unequal exchanges originally created, and now maintains, this gradation of classes—this division of society into a class to pay rent, and a class to receive and enjoy it ; and there will always be a class of workers and a class of idlers, and the gain of the last will always be the loss of the first, so long as men thus exchange unequally with each other. There never can, from the very nature of things, be equal rights and equal laws in a state of things like this ; for the

very spirit of inequality and injustice exists in every institution and governs every transaction. Under present
arrangements, every thing goes from the creator of wealth
—the working man—step by step, and paying tribute to
every other class, until it arrives in the shape of £20,000
a year at some capitalist or proprietor—who takes this
money, not in exchange for his labour—not in *exchange*
for anything—but it is given to him because the usages of
society, without the least shadow of reason or justice, have
ordained that it shall be so !

No other than the present social system could by any
possibility create and perpetuate the gross injustice which
is now inflicted upon the great body of exchangers—the
working class. They are plundered on all sides, and preyed
upon by all other classes. They form, like their parent
earth, a common pasture-ground, on which all crawling
and creeping things may feed and fatten.

Nothing but a total change of system—an equalising of
labour and exchanges—can alter this state of things for
the better, and ensure men a true equality of rights. These
examples of the working of the present system may
likewise serve to explain the manner in which the system
ought to work. For instance—the £20,000 received by
any proprietor or capitalist, for rent or interest, is a part
of the surplus of production over consumption—it is as
so much clear profit, to be enjoyed by man as a reward for
his toil. In the case of the landed proprietor, the parties
more immediately concerned in the production of the
£20,000 rent—although the working men of all denominations indirectly contribute to it—are, first of all, the
labourers of the farmer, who receive an annual £20 or £30
for their labour of ten or twelve hours a-day ; then come
the farmers, each of whom, perhaps, clears £200 a-year
for his labour of six hours a day ; and the landholder receives the £20,000 a-year for no labour whatever. It
matters not how many working men may assist in creating
this sum—it stands apart from them, and is not enjoyed
by them ; but were the two great laws of universal labour
and equal exchanges in force, this £20,000 of rent or profit
would be, as it ought to be, equally divided amongst and
enjoyed by the parties assisting in its production. The
twelve hours of the one portion, and the six hours of the
other, and the perfect idleness of the last, would, if thus

equalized, inflict but very moderate labour upon all concerned; while the various sums of £30, £200, and £20,000, if likewise equally divided—as they would be by a system of equal exchanges—would at once place the working man in that position, and afford him all those advantages, to which he is so justly entitled by his labour and his usefulness.

The same injustice which is inflicted upon the agricultural labourers by the present system, is suffered, likewise, by the working men of all trades. The labour in all is thus unequal, and the remuneration is thus unequal. The gain of the class of capitalists and employers is always the loss of the working class.

Let, then, the working men of every grade and every employment ponder but for one moment upon their situation as it is, and as it may be and ought to be. It is in their power to alter, at once, the whole character of the present corrupt and unjust system of society; and when the cause of ill is thus removed, the various effects now observable will be known and felt no longer. They can change their inordinate toil, and poverty, and discontentment, into comparative recreation, and wealth, and joy. The movement will have no danger in it—the advantages to be obtained are not the creations of a distempered brain. The producers have but to make an effort—and by them must every effort for their own redemption be made—and their chains will be snapped asunder for ever. They know that their labour, with the assistance of machinery, creates wealth of the annual value of about £500,000,000, and they know, also, that nearly two thirds of this vast sum is absorbed by the rich idler, and the half-employed and mis-employed tradesman. Why should not society be constituted so that double this amount may be created, and the toil of the workman at the same time be decreased one half? To attain this end, two things only are necessary— capital and labour. With regard to the first, all the accumulations of capital—the machinery and implements—by which the creation of wealth is now effected, exist around us on every side; and it will only require the same application of labour the next year, to produce similar results to those which have been accomplished during the past year. By labour, the present accumulations of machinery and implements may be indefinitely increased; and, as they are increased, enjoyments will be increased and labour will

be diminished. As for the labour, it is within the bones
and sinews of the producers. Thus all the materials of
success are in existence, and it will only require a proper
combination and organization of the power which the productive classes possess, to effect all that the heart of man
can wish for. Surely the sufferings and the wrongs endured by the working man for four thousand years, under
all systems of religion and all forms of government, will
have taught him that no mere governmental change can
give him that equality of rights and enjoyments which unfettered justice would award to him. No such changes will
have the power to exalt the producers above their present
degraded level, for *they can have no effect upon their position with respect to other classes.* They will still be the
mere footstool—still the dregs of society—to be thrown
aside, and left to rot, when their usefulness has passed
away. Such has ever been the fate of the workmen's order,
and such it always must be, so long as society is divided
into employers and employed—and the last are placed, by
their position, at the mercy of the first.

It is only by acting upon those principles of justice and
equality which we have been considering, that man can do
away with all tyranny, all poverty, and all wrong. No
other than these principles are capable of uniting families
and nations into one vast fraternity ; for, from their nature,
they strike at once at all that has hitherto made men disunited—*Inequality of Labour—Inequality of Wealth—
Inequality of Power.*

We have now viewed, side by side, our governmental
and our social wrongs—we have placed in different scales
those burthens imposed upon the productive classes by a
monarchical form of government, and those which owe
their origin to the present social system, of which monarchy and aristocracy are no more than natural off-shoots.
A further consideration of the case will convince us, that
the remedy for the greater evil may be just as easily obtained as the remedy for the least ; while, in respect to
the advantages to be derived from each, there can be no
comparison.

Having thus probed the evil to its core, who can be surprised at the discontentment of the toiling millions ? Who
will start at their fierce and deep-breathed imprecations on
a system which yearly plunders them of wealth of the value

of three hundred millions of pounds sterling—a system which compels them to produce this vast amount for the enjoyment of those who treat them with derision and contempt? Shall the working man everlastingly toil and sweat, and be for ever thus plundered, and degraded, and trampled upon? Is it to pamper the unholy pride of those who thus abuse him, that the infancy of his little ones is seared and blighted amid the foul and steamy air of cotton mills and factories?—that his own manhood is bowed down with the premature age produced by excessive toil? Shall his complaints be always hushed by the roaring of artillery— his indignant heart stilled by the thrust of the bayonet— his upbraidings stifled in dungeons? If he would have things to continue thus, let him still go on, as he has heretofore done, drivelling and dreaming of relief from legislators and governments—from classes and castes, who, deriving their wealth and their supremacy from his toil and abasement, know him only as a bondman or an inferior.

If the working man would change this state of things, he must look no longer to mere *effects*—he must at once destroy the *cause* from which his sufferings arise. Equal rights and equal laws cannot, from the nature of things, exist in connection with unequal duties, unequal wealth, and unequal exchanges. It is not a form of government which the working class must blame for their wrongs, but the system of society from which that form springs—it is not their oppressors and murderers whom they must curse, for it is the system which makes them oppressors and murderers— it is not the rich and the grasping capitalist whom they must abuse and persecute for their poverty, but they must alter the system which makes one man rich and another man poor.

When our governmental and our social burthens are thus separately examined, how insignificant appears the merely monetary saving which a change in the form of our government will enable us to effect, when compared with that which a change in our social system will produce. Even admitting that its cost may be greatly lessened, what will it matter to the working man how much is saved in the expense of government, if he have not the enjoyment of such saving? And it has been proved, upon principles which cannot be controverted, that his very position in society debars him from receiving much, if any, relief from reduced taxation. The wealth which the working class would create, and the portion of it which they would enjoy, would not be affected by changes in government—it would still be determined by causes, and be dependent on classes, that no political power would enable the producer of it to control.

Let the working classes of the United Kingdom, then, if they can, hesitate to decide between two remedies—a social and a governmental remedy—the one of which will save them £300,000,000 millions a year, and enable them to produce everything they want by the labour of six or eight hours a day; while the other, if carried to its utmost extent—the subversion of the monarchy and the institution of a republic—cannot, from the very constitution of society, save *them* even twenty millions a year, and will compel them to toil on, in utter hopelessness and poverty, until the race of man becomes extinct. A change of the social system will be a perspective as well as a present advantage. It will affect all future generations of men as well as ourselves; and all the benefits which we shall derive from such change will increase, instead of substracting from, the enjoyments of those who come after us. A system based upon the laws of Universal Labour and Equal Exchanges can alone do all men justice, and make society truly "a state presenting an uninterrupted succession of advantages for *all* its members."

"He who hath wife and child, hath given hostages to Fortune;" and ought not Fortune, likewise, to give him hostages? The toils of the past and the present should always secure to the working man and his family the enjoyment of the future. But the present system offers the worn-out workman no enjoyment—and no alleviation of unmerited distress and poverty, except in connection with degradation and hardship. And, again, what kind of a welcome and a shelter does society at large now offer to the wife and the children of the expiring working man—to those for whom he has worn out his strength in unremitting toil? None. They wander over the earth as poor and pennyless beggars, or, like criminals, they are confined in pauper prisons. The mother becomes separated from the children, and the children are parted from each other—the chords which bound their young hearts together are snapped asunder for ever—and they wander

over the face of the earth homeless and friendless, despised
and enslaved because they are ignorant, and disregarded
and ill-treated because they are poor. Is it to be wondered
at that these unfavourable circumstances should do their
work—that misery and prostitution is the portion of the
one sex, and the transport-ship or the gallows the fate of
the other ! Even the small and miserable pittance which
grinding Capital permits tired Labour and unprotected
childhood still to enjoy, by means of what are termed
" poor-laws," will shortly be withheld. These miserable
substitutes for justice, inefficient and almost worthless as
they are, will soon exist only in name ; for it has been
acknowledged by those who drink up the very life-blood of
the working class, and who are now experimenting as to
the length which human endurance of oppression can go,
that " poor-laws" are a great and growing evil, which must
by some means be got rid of.

Look at the present social system on whatever side and
in whatever light we may, we behold but one compact mass
of deformity and depravity. If Tyranny would revel in
the wealth of one people and the blood of another, then is
this the proper system for Tyranny: if Priestcraft would
enslave and stultify the human mind, and manufacture
soulless tools for despotism, then is this the proper system
for Priestcraft : if the commission of crime, and the practice of vice, and the waste of labour, be the chief ends for
which men unite in society, then is this a proper social
system !

It is for all men and all nations to declare whether
tyranny and priestcraft, robbery and ignorance, wholesale
murder and intellectual depravation, shall any longer reign
triumphant over truth and justice. The question will in
future be determined neither by despotism nor its twin-
brother. The £300,000,000 which the working classes
annually lose by this system, vast as is the amount, is the
least part of their loss ; for they are likewise plundered
of all those high enjoyments which alone and exclusively
make existence to be brute or human.

Thus, whether we regard a governmental change and
the establishment of political equality either as a means or
as an end—as a step whereby to obtain the good we seek
for, or as constituting of itself the actual good—both
reason and experience join in shewing us the utter worth-

lessness of all such changes, either as means or as ends. Reason tells us that there is no cure for an effect while the cause is left untouched. Experience points to the United States' republic—which is politically all that we have heretofore desired, and more than we have ever hoped to obtain—and we behold there the imperious tyrant and the chained slave—the moneyed monarch and the famished beggar—the bankrupt capitalist and the unemployed working man :—we behold, in fact, every wrong and every misery and every vice with which we are familiar here. As an end, then, political equality is there a failure—a shadow, cold, cheerless, and unsubstantial as the northern meteors to the freezing traveller. As a means, also, it is there a failure, as perceptible and as proved as that two and three are not six; for the political power of the working classes of the United States is, of itself, as incompetent to effect their deliverance from the social wrongs they endure in common with us, as would be a wooden file to cut away the fetters from their Ethiopian fellow-slaves. The working classes of all nations suffer a common wrong, and they require a common remedy. That remedy is not merely the possession of political power, as political power now is —that remedy is not morality, as morality now is—that remedy is not religion, as religion now is—but it is a remedy which can be derived only from the establishment of FIRST PRINCIPLES.

CHAPTER VII.

THE INUTILITY OF THE REMEDIES AT PRESENT
CONTENDED FOR.

THE preceding chapters have been devoted almost exclusively to a consideration of the wrongs endured by the productive classes of the United Kingdom, and the cause of those wrongs ; but no particular remedy has yet been examined, nor has any plan been pointed out, beyond the general recommendation to establish First Principles. We have considered these principles, and they have taught us, that the rights of all men are equal—that all men ought to labour—that the earth is the common property of all its inhabitants. We have looked, likewise, at the institution of human society ; the true intention of which is, to neutralise that trifling inequality of bodily and mental powers in men which nature has created, and to equalise the benefits which a wise and judicious application of the varied powers of men may call into existence. We have also regarded the three conditions laid down by the political economists—" that there shall be labour—that there shall be accumulations—that there shall be exchanges." These conditions are themselves based on the acknowledgment of human equality ; and they merely shew the manner in which first principles are to be acted upon, and equality of rights maintained, in a state of society. A consideration of the subject has taught us, however, that all the wrongs and evils which man has suffered since his creation, are to be attributed solely to the infraction of these conditions by individuals and classes. We have learnt, that unless there be labour, there can be no capital or accumulations—unless there be accumulations, there cannot be exchanges ; and from this dependency it follows, that he who has not laboured, and who will not labour, cannot be an exchanger, for he can have nothing to exchange, there being nothing exchangeable but labour, or the produce of labour. To make this principle of exchange subservient to the intention of society and the happiness of man, exchanges must always be equal, or the gain of one man will ever be the loss of another. A consideration of the subject of exchanges has shewn us, that inequality of exchanges, and not inequality of political power, generates inequality of condition, and the gradation of classes, and divides society into rich and poor; and that, so long as there are unequal exchanges amongst men, there must be idlers and labourers — there must be rich and poor — as the poverty of the last is a necessary consequence of the wealth of the first. We have seen, likewise, that inequality of condition, and the division of society into capitalists and producers—into employers and employed—leaves the last class entirely at the mercy of the first;—that such dependence necessarily dooms the working class, no matter what may be their intelligence or their morality, to a state of hopeless slavery to other classes, and keeps them in perpetual poverty or the fear of poverty;—and that, therefore, inequality of condition is, from its nature, subversive of all equality of rights and laws, whatever may be the form of government instituted, and whatever may be the mere political power possessed by the people. The truth of this conclusion was made manifest to us by a consideration of the condition of the working classes in ancient and modern times, and under republican as well as monarchical governments; for we find that every wrong which is suffered by the working class of the United Kingdom at the present day is likewise suffered in degree by their brethren in republican America, and has been endured by the whole of their order since the very commencement of history. It has been seen, too, as well as it has long been felt, that the wrongs of the working class of the United Kingdom are not imaginary, as their enemies would have them to believe; but that they are as substantial as the annual sum of nearly three hundred millions of pounds sterling can make them,—and this, too, apart from, and independent of, the wrongs originating from the particular form of their government.

These various facts and considerations plainly prove, that the question to be decided must in reality henceforth be,—shall we have a change of system, or no change whatever?   Will the working classes of the United Kingdom direct their future efforts to the attainment of a social remedy or a governmental nonentity?—will they keep on for ever hammering at the *effect,* or strike at once at the *cause?*—will they totally subvert the present system, and thereby do away at once with all the inequality and injustice and bad government which this system generates; or will they, by successive and endless governmental changes, merely alter the appearance and vary the form of the Great Wrong—leaving untouched its very essence, and suffering, with unmitigated severity, every species of misery and injustice which that essence can engender? Inequality of condition is the direct producer of every social ill and governmental wrong; and equality of exchanges only can do away with inequality of condition, and bestow on, and preserve to all, equality of rights.

Thus stands the question, stripped of those multifarious mysticisms in which cunning has so well assisted ignorance to envelop it.   We here see the question of right and wrong as a whole, as well as in its parts; and, instead of wandering about in an interminable labyrinth of petty wrongs and petty remedies, curing old sores by inflicting new wounds, we can stand as it were apart from the entire system.   We can survey it on every side, and, knowing the source of the wrong, shall thus be no longer misled and disappointed by those infallible men and infallible measures, that have for so many centuries begotten Hope by their promises, only to murder it by their performances.

Long have the working classes of the United Kingdom suffered the various wrongs and burthens which we have been considering; and numerous have been the remedies proposed and tried for the purpose of changing such a state of things for the better.   All, however, have either failed entirely, or they have succeeded but partially, and but for a moment.   The people have tried social remedies and political remedies—local remedies and general remedies: they have entered into benefit societies, and trades' unions, and political associations—they have formed combinations among themselves, more or less formidable in regard to numbers and to wealth; but one scheme after another has been abandoned, and exchanged for something else that had, perhaps, been thrown aside a generation before.

With regard to these remedies, one principle or character pervades the whole—a blind and unreasoning attempt to do away with effects, and at the same time suffering causes to remain sacred and untouched.   There is a leak in the ship; and all these various intermediate remedies relate, not to the stopping up of such leak, but to the getting out of the water which is running in ; and there is no lack of shallow-pated drivellers who know so little of the nature and relation of things, as to gravely discuss, in effect—not whether the leak shall be stopped, but whether it is better to throw out one bucket full of water in a given time, or two half-buckets.

The various political associations and unions which have at times been formed to benefit the working class, by obtaining for them particular governmental changes, have done nothing whatever towards bettering the condition of the masses, by removing their poverty or increasing their enjoyments.   The great majority of the leading advocates of mere political changes have ever taken a narrow and one-sided view of the nature of man, and his wants, and his capabilities.   They look at the world simply as it is—comprised of an oppressed working class, and an oppressing governing class.   They appear not to conceive the possibility of human society being constituted otherwise than as they find it ; and therefore all their political remedies have no more in view than the partial amelioration of the condition of the working class *as a working class*—a class confessedly doomed, by the unalterable nature of things, to be the servants or the slaves of other classes.   Thus, all the political remedies heretofore sought for and obtained—as they did not go to the causes which had created a mere working class, and had made that class oppressed and degraded—were necessarily ineffectual in removing the oppression and degradation complained of.

It would have been far better for the people of the present day, if the politicians of former times, when setting themselves to legislate for rich men, *as such,* and poor men, *as such,* had thought of inquiring how it came to pass that some men were rich and some were poor ; or how it happened that one class toiled away, generation after generation, without becoming any richer, and the other class ate, drank, and were merry, generation after generation, without becoming less rich. The real evil which the working classes endure, and the one from which they want to be relieved, is their incessant toil, and their poverty, and the oppression exercised upon them to obtain their wealth ; for the wrong is whole and indivisible, the governmental part arising out of, and being determined by, the social part. It has been clearly shewn, however, that this toil and poverty is not dependent on form of government—that it is caused by inequality of labour and inequality of exchanges—and that, therefore, it could not possibly be removed by any merely governmental change whatever.

Instead of rightly considering their own wrongs, and devising and adopting proper remedies, the working classes have too confidingly left their cause to the guardianship and direction of men who, from their position in society, and the particular prejudices connected with that position, were necessarily weak champions and blind guides. Such men have almost always taught the workman to look for relief to political changes and governmental reforms ; but the majority of these advisers have not belonged to the working class, and therefore, not knowing what working men have suffered, or how they have felt and thought, it was not likely that they should know what kind of a remedy was wanted. Besides, even if these leaders of the people had known the true wrong and the true remedy — if they had seen that the poverty and toil of the poor was a necessary consequence of the wealth and the idleness of the rich—their very position in society, connected as they are with rich men, and living as they do upon rents and profits, would have made them hostile to the interests and opposed to the wishes of the working class. The suprema-cy of the one can exist only by the degradation of the other —this supremacy was never intended by politicians to be subverted—and therefore the men and their measures were of a piece, neither of them going to the wrong, and neither of them pointing to the remedy.

The insufficiency of political measures to remedy social grievances, was long since seen by thousands of the working classes — they had a conception, although not a clear one, that the gain of the capitalist was the loss of the pro-ducer—and therefore they sought relief by the institution of trade societies and trades' unions. The trades' unions, although constituted differently from the political unions, and working by other means, had the same ultimate object in view as the latter, namely, the *partial* amelioration of the condition of the working class *as a working class*. But while the political unions sought to obtain benefit in a gradual and indirect manner, by reducing taxation, and by other means, the trades' unions endeavoured to accomplish the wished-for end immediately and directly, by compelling the capitalist and the employer to refund, in the shape of increased wages, a part of that vast amount of wealth which they were annually drawing from the working classes: they were endeavouring, in fact, to act somewhat upon the principle of equal exchanges, by obtaining the full value of their labour.

The great body of the working classes believed that their late trades' unions would be omnipotent in effecting their deliverance from the dominion of the capitalist ; for a more powerful engine was never made use of by the producers. From there being many trades united together, and supporting each other, when one struck a blow at tyranny, that blow fell with the accumulated monetary force of the whole mass. But, whether victorious or defeated, the workman was alike involved in losses and in difficulties—all his efforts for the permanent bettering of his condition were ineffectual—and this vast confederation was at length broken up, and dissolved into its primitive trade societies. These have continued, at times, a desultory and unequal contest with capital—sometimes with partial success, but oftener with defeat and ruin. The capitalist and the employer have always ultimately been too strong for them ; and trades' unions have become, amongst the enemies of the working class, a bye-word of caution or contempt—a record of the weakness of Labour when opposed to Capital—an indestructible memento of the evil working of the present system in regard to the two great classes which now compose society.

Many reasons are given to account for the dissolution and destruction of the trades' unions. There was in numerous cases abject poverty amongst multitudes of the members ; and, in some instances, there was treachery and robbery on the part of leaders, which naturally begot suspicion and distrust. Much tyranny and injustice was inflicted by both sides on individual working men and individual capitalists, and much precious wealth wasted by each to no good purpose. But, whatever may have been the more immediate and apparent cause of failure, it is certain, from the nature of the wrong, that it was not possible for the remedy of the trades' unions to succeed any better than the remedy of the politicians. Neither party went far enough. The same primitive cause has thwarted the endeavours and blighted the energies of both. The evils to be remedied flowed naturally from, and were dependent upon, the social system and the principle of unequal exchanges; and as neither political nor trades' unions touched the system or the principle, they could not possibly touch the wrong connected with them.

Unsatisfied alike with the result obtained by both political and trades' unions, a portion of the working classes have vainly endeavoured to obtain relief through the instrumentality of some governmental enactment which should restrict their hours of labour. Much has been said for and against this limitation scheme; but if any such be ever carried into effect, it will be as useless, and as ineffectual in permanently bettering the condition of the working class, as any other merely governmental change. Any such remedy will alter the relative position of the master and the man no more than the political or trades' unions' remedies will—any such remedy will reduce neither the numbers of the rich nor the poor—and therefore it is not possible that any such remedy should cure the evils which this relative position and this division inflict upon the workman.

We have already seen that the capitalist—the employer —by his very position in society, as the purchaser and controller of the labour of the working class, has it in his power to suck from them, whether they will or not, the greater part of the wealth which they produce. Under present arrangements, Labour is at the mercy of Capital. If, therefore, for working twelve or sixteen hours a day, many operatives receive only 12s. or 16s. a week as their share of the wealth created, it must follow, that any reduction in their hours of labour will be succeeded by a corresponding reduction in their share of produce. It is the number of idle and unprofitable capitalists and proprietors that the working classes now have to support, which imposes upon them such excessive toil, and reduces their wages to the miserable pittance which so many thousands of them receive. The true remedy, therefore, and the only remedy, is, to reduce the number of the capitalists and proprietors, that more wealth may be enjoyed by the working class. If the present arrangements of society—the accursed system of unequal exchanges—enables one-fifth of the nation to seize upon one-half of all that is produced, it is self-evident that no *decrease* in the amount of production —no reduction in the hours of labour—can at all *increase* the share of the working class. The share of wealth which they in either case receive and enjoy, will be governed solely by the number of idlers they are compelled to maintain; and, therefore, the less the wealth which the working classes produce, the less will be the share received by them. Thus, if they work fewer hours they will produce less wealth—there will necessarily be less to divide between themselves and the capitalists—and the result of such reduction in the hours of labour will be,—not that the working classes will receive a greater share, but that both they and the capitalists will receive less. This principle applies generally to the working class, as a class; but the circumstances which determine the hours which shall be worked and the prices which shall be paid in particular trades, arise from causes dependent on demand and supply —causes which, under the present system, no legislative measure can beneficially effect.

It must never be forgotten by the working class, when reviewing their wrongs and devising remedies, that their warfare is not against men, but against a system—that they are fighting not against the capitalists, as individuals, nor against capital itself, but *against the present mode of applying capital—against that system which gives to irresponsible individuals the power of grinding masses of labour between masses of capital.* There is no remedy for this, except a change of system. Without such a change, the cause of the redemption of the working class is a hopeless one !

It would be a waste of time to recapitulate the whole of the various schemes which have been at times devised to cure, or at least to account for, the present state of things. The capitalists and the political economists have not been idle in this latter service; and amongst the many incomprehensible and contradictory doctrines which they have

brought forth to account for much work existing in connection with little wages—and to account, also for some
men being poor, and some men being rich—some doing all the work, and others receiving almost all the benefit
—is the fallacy of demand and supply. The economists
most methodically place the capital and the capitalists on
the one side, and the work and the working class on the
other. When it happens that there are more working
men than can be employed by the capitalist, the former are
told that there is a "glut of labour" in the market.
Work is difficult to procure, and, if obtained, it must be
done for less money than was before received. Under the
present arrangements of society, there is always such a
"glut of labour," as it is called, in almost every trade and
profession—there is ever a greater or less number of men
only partially employed, or altogether unemployed, and
thus placed on the very verge of starvation. The economists tell us that this state of things is not dependent
upon, nor in any way connected with, form of government; but that it happens necessarily and unavoidably,
and can only be removed by the course of proceeding
which they point out. They say that there is only a certain quantity of capital or money in the country capable
of being applied to the purposes of production; that this
money, therefore, being thus limited, can only employ a
certain number of labourers at 20s. a week, or double that
number at 10s., or four times that number at 5s.:—that
it from hence necessarily follows, that the more labourers
there are, the worse it will be for them; and, therefore,
the only remedy for this inequality between labour and
capital is, for some of the labourers to "go out of the market,"—to keep down their numbers—to emigrate, or die
off by disease and starvation, until they are again within
the range of Capital, and there are rather fewer of them
than are wanted. When this takes place, say the economists, Capital and Labour will maintain their natural
equilibrium, and the competition among the capitalists will
raise to their proper level the wages of those working men
who remain; for, say they, it is the competition amongst
the working classes to obtain employment, which now
brings down the value of labour; and, so long as there are
a greater number of working men than the capitalists have
money to employ, it is beyond the power of man, either by

means of trades' unions, or short-time bills, or governmental changes of any description, to alleviate, permanently, the condition of the working class.

Upon a slight examination, this explanation of the economists appears a very rational mode of accounting for the
present distress, and the compulsory idleness of so many
able working men as are now wandering about unemployed;
but it does not account for the present gradation of classes,
nor would it, if carried out to its utmost extent, relieve the
working class from that enormous load which now presses
them into the earth. This remedy finds them slaves, and
it would leave them so. It is very apparent to every man,
that if there be a certain quantity of work to be done,—
suppose the digging of a canal—and a specified and
sufficient sum of money to pay for it, and just so many
labourers as there are shovels for, the whole concern will
go on well enough while the several parts are thus nicely
adjusted to each other; it is also evident, that if there be
twice as many labourers as there are shovels and wages
for, half of these labourers must remain idle, or the whole
of them work half-time, and receive half-pay. The same
principle is perpetually seen in operation in one trade or
another. But even admitting that the deficiency of money
is the true cause of the non-employment of these most
unwilling idlers, is there no other remedy than that of
starving them to death or transporting them? Will it not
be as rational and as practicable, now that the labourers
are here, to increase the shovels to the wants of the workers,
as it will be to beat down the labourers to the level of the
shovels? If the economists cannot answer this question,
it shall be answered for them.

The doctrine of a "glut of labour," although apparently
borne out by facts, is in reality as false and as unsupported
as the veriest fiction that ever imposed upon the credulity
of mankind. There never yet has been, and there is not
now, and there cannot be for thousands of years, such a
thing as a "glut of labour;" and a positive contradiction
is involved in the assertion that there is such a glut.
All human appliances of labour are intended to procure
for man houses, food, clothes, and other necessaries and
luxuries; for these things can be obtained only by labour. It is evident, therefore, that one of two things is
necessary to the condition of a glut of labour. We all

have a sufficiency of every necessary and luxury for consumption—and, therefore, a superabundance of labour in
consequence of repletion of wealth;—or else, wanting some
or all of these things, the raw material of which they are
composed is not in sufficient quantity to employ all our
labour,—and thus there is a glut, from the circumstance
of our having nothing to work upon.

It need not be asked whether every person in the United
Kingdom has a sufficiency of the various necessaries and luxuries which labour calls into existence. If all have enough,
and to spare, then is there truly a glut of labour ; and
the working class may sit down and enjoy themselves until some of this abundance is consumed. But if every person have not such a sufficiency of these good things, and
there nevertheless be plenty of the raw material to work
upon, then there cannot truly be a glut of labour. The
desire for certain things exists within us—the material of
these things is around us—the labour requisite to work up
this material is under our own control ; and, until all
their wants are satisfied, or the treasures of the earth exhausted, it is a palpable untruth to tell the working classes
that there is a "glut of labour;" for the half-clothed
backs and hungry bellies of many a suffering thousand tell
them, again and again, that they are in want of everything
which labour can procure. The system must be altered
which sets their labour in motion and keeps it moving ;
and then, and not till then, will the triple contradiction of
too many hands, too much raw material, and too little
produce to enjoy, be done away with !

To affirm, as the economists do, that there are too many
agricultural labourers, while there is at the same time
plenty of unemployed land, and thousands of operatives
are in want of bread—or that there are too many
operatives and artizans, while millions of the community
are in want of clothes, houses, and other necessaries,—is
so glaring a contradiction—so strange an anomaly—as to
strike at once the most obtuse understanding ; and if there
were not innumerable instances before the eyes of every
one, it would be difficult to believe even in the possibility
of the existence of such a state of things. At the present
time, multitudes of these various classes of producers are
compelled to remain in idleness and impoverishment, while
each man is in want of the very things which his unem-

ployed neighbour can produce! He who knows how to grow corn must stand still and starve, because the capitalist has the land—he who can make cloth must go barebacked, because the capitalists have the wool, and the mills, and the machinery. All these contradictions—all this want of employment and this poverty—arise from that system which places accumulations of capital in the hands of individuals and classes—from that system which makes one class dependent upon another for the means of labour, and thus, necessarily, for the means of life and happiness. It has always been thus with the working classes—under republics as well as monarchies—and, under the present system of unequal exchanges it always will be so, whether they be illiterate or educated, immoral or religious, temperate or debauched.

Is there, then, *no* remedy for these evils—for this complicated idleness, and wretchedness, and excessive toil of such vast numbers of artisans and agriculturists? Can nothing be done to enable one class to grow corn, and other classes to produce their respective commodities—to provide sufficient employment and ample remuneration for all men, in all trades—that every member of society may be not only well supported and educated, but likewise well provided for in age? We have seen that all the merely governmental changes contended for by the politicians—whether having reference to extended voting, or reduction in the hours of labour, or other similar measures—will not do it, or they would have done it in the United States. We have seen that the trades' unions, however powerful and well conducted, cannot do it, or they would have gone on and conquered. We have seen that the remedy proposed by the political economists cannot do it, as the means are not only impracticable, but likewise totally inadequate to obtain the end desired, even were they carried out to their utmost extent. The economists, like the politicians, know only of the capitalist, as such, and the working man, as such. All their remedies have reference only to the present system of inequality and injustice—that system which, by unequal exchanges, robs every working man of two-thirds of his just earnings, to keep up the supremacy and the wealth of those who are not working men—that system which, being thus constituted and maintained, will spontaneously and necessarily produce governmental institutions imbued with its own spirit, and characteristic of its own vileness and depravity. As, therefore, all the evils of which we complain result from the present system, and none of these numerous remedies touch the system itself, it is not in the nature of things that any of them should be successful; or that they should ever do more than drive in the evil at one part, that it may break out with increased virulence at another. There is no remedy apart from the destruction of the wrong; and the subversion of the present social system must be accomplished, or the evils which arise from this system can never be eradicated.

CHAPTER VIII.

THE REQUISITES OF A SOCIAL SYSTEM.

THE retrospect which has been taken of the character and tendency of the present social system, has afforded abundant proof that there is within this system a principle which must ever doom four-fifths of the community to political and social damnation, under every modification of religion and every form of government. The reviewal entered into has shewn us not only some of the many failures which have followed the efforts of man to alter the present state of things for the better, but it has at the same time made us acquainted with the cause of these failures, and has thus placed the future destiny of man within his own hands. We have seen that this system spontaneously generates inequality of wealth and inequality of power, and that it therefore is, and always must be, subversive of every just political institution and all equality of social rights which may be at any time established. We have discovered, likewise, that inequality of wealth, and the gradation of classes, is produced and maintained by inequality of exchanges; and, however inequality of exchanges may have been originally induced, observation and experience unite in shewing that the principle is now perpetuated by the existence of *inequality of wealth in connection with the gradation of classes,* or the division of society into capitalists and producers. Inequality of possessions, when considered by itself, and unconnected with inequality of exchanges and the gradation of classes, is not a great evil. To the man whose labour has procured him two suits of clothes, it matters not whether another person has two or four suits, provided this second man have obtained his superfluity by means of exchanging his own labour equally against the labour of some other person. An absolute equality of possessions can no more exist among men, than an absolute equality in regard to strength and stature. In every state of society, there will always be some kind of individual and personal property ; and difference of character will ever make such property both unequal and varied.

Having traced our social and political evils to their source, and discovered the principle on which they hinge, it now remains to be seen whether or not the opposite principle of equal exchanges contain within itself the remedy ; and whether it be practicable, by particular social arrangements, to establish and act upon this principle.

It has been clearly shewn that man has nothing to exchange except his labour, or the produce of his labour ; and that, therefore, when men exchange products with each other, they merely give, as it were, labour for labour. Thus, where the raw materials of two articles are of the same value, and an equal portion of labour has been bestowed upon them, strict justice requires that the two should exchange equally against each other. Where things are thus of equal value, and they are exchanged unequally, the gain of one exchanger must ever be the loss of another, and ultimately there will be generated rich and poor, and laws and institutions will be framed to constitute the first a wiser, a better, and a more privileged order than the last. But where equal exchanges are maintained, the gain of one man cannot be the loss of another ; for every exchange is then simply a *transfer*, and not a *sacrifice*, of labour and wealth. Thus, although, under a social system based on equal exchanges, a parsimonious man may become rich, his wealth will be no more than the accumulated produce of his own labour. He may exchange his wealth, or he may give it to others who will exchange it, for an equal value of the wealth of other persons ; but a rich man cannot continue wealthy for any length of time after he has ceased to labour. Under equality of exchanges, wealth cannot have, as it now has, a procreative and apparently self-generating power, such as replenishes all waste from consumption ; for, unless it be renewed by labour, wealth, when once consumed, is given up for ever. That which is now called profit and interest cannot exist, as such, in connection with equality of exchanges ; for producer and distributor would be alike remunerated, and the sum total of their labour would determine the value of the article created and brought to the hands of the consumer.

The principle of equal exchanges, therefore, must, from its very nature, ensure universal labour—it will consequently be destructive of that great social ulcer, the maintenance of one class at the expense of another: it will prevent the division of society into classes and castes—it must therefore maintain social and political equality of rights: it will do away with the want of work, the excessive toil, and the hopeless poverty which now exist—and it will at the same time destroy all the moral and physical evils induced and maintained by such a state of things.

This is all that is contended for and all that is desired—it has been clearly shewn that this result can never be obtained in any system founded upon the principle of unequal exchanges—and it has now to be determined what social arrangements must be instituted to establish and maintain equality of exchanges, or as near an approximation to the principle as the trifling inequalities amongst men will admit of. An approach to truth is all that can be made by human beings; for abstract perfection will never be found either in man or his institutions.

There is in man an instinctive principle which perpetually impels him to seek the company and the assistance of his kind. There are feelings within him which must have vent—feelings which yearn for communion with something after their own nature—and, wherever man is cut off from all sympathetic connection with his fellows, he will find a companion even among the animals which constitute his food. On this will he bestow a portion of those feelings which he has been debarred from exercising towards his own species—he will partake alike of its pleasures and its troubles—and the caresses returned by his dumb associate will speak strongly though silently to his heart. This principle of love exists throughout creation, and, by successive links, holds in connection all that is animate and all that is inanimate. There is no such thing as solitude, or silence, or isolation.

In considering, then, a social system, it requires no speculation as to the reasons or the advantages which originally induced society. It is sufficient that society exists and that, in some form or other, it always will exist. It' is nothing less than a state of society, if two human beings hold communion with each other—it is no more than society if there be congregated together two hundred millions.

All human beings, whether in or out of society, united together in larger or smaller communities,, are imperatively governed by the indestructible but directible principle of self-love. By particular social arrangements, this principle may be made to benefit an individual in a direct manner, without benefiting his fellows—it may be made to benefit an individual in a direct manner, and at the same time benefit others—it may be made to benefit an individual indirectly, through the medium of others. The first mode of operation is incompatible with personal safety and social peace—the second is unfavourable to the growth of individual charity and general love—the third contains within itself the elements of safety, and charity, and peace. The true excellence of a social system, therefore, will depend upon the manner in which it brings into action and governs the principle of self-love, so that society at large may suffer as few ills and enjoy as many advantages as possible.

Under present arrangements, the principle of self-love in every individual is left at liberty to work any way and every way, as uncontrolled circumstances may determine; and from hence arises that discordant and conflicting jumble of interests—that admixture of good and bad institutions and practices—that unintermitted warfare between individuals and classes—which has so long tired the patience and grieved the heart of man. The present social arrangements admit of a non-producing aristocracy, and benefit that class without benefiting the producers—and in this there is evil and wrong : these arrangements create and maintain a commercial and trading aristocracy, and benefit that class as ten and the producers but as one—and in this there must be political misrule as well as social injustice : and all such arrangements, as they do not benefit indirectly, but plunder and enslave directly, the vast mass of the producers, must always be subversive of everything like safety, or charity, or love.

But, besides the proper government of self-love, and as a means to this end, a social system must contain the requisite arrangements for the production and equable distribution of an unlimited quantity of wealth—for the perfect security of persons and property—and for the physical moral, and intellectual cultivation of all its members. The present system is almost destitute of every one of these requisites: it places an unnatural limit to the production of wealth, and distributes in a grossly unjust manner that which is produced: persons and property are as unsafe from attack and spoliation as they can be under any circumstances, for the principle of social love is cramped and confined within the smallest limits in which it can exist: the physical, moral, and intellectual culture of the best among us is anything but what it ought to be; while the powers of whole sections of the community are totally neglected, and circumstances are left at liberty to produce adult human beings varying in intellect from the oyster to the elephant, and actuated by a charity and love akin to that of the tiger and the hyena.

Our present system is deficient in all these requisites; and reason alone would be capable of predicting all those social evils which experience hourly brings to view. But unseemly as is a state of things like this, and unfavourable as it ever must be to those high aspirations after human exaltation which cheer on the philanthropist in his thankless labours, it is well to know that there is in man no intellectual depravation which may not be elevated and refined—no brutal propensity which may not be tamed and humanized.

To suppose that a high elevation and a general uniformity of character can exist amongst the people of a nation, would, at the present day, excite only derision. When philosophically viewed, however, such a desideratum does not lie without the verge of possibility. It will be universally admitted, that, even under the present system, much as there is of evil and little as there is of good, all persons are not equally ignorant, nor equally disposed to violence and crime. If a perfect uniformity in respect to character and actions now prevailed among men, there would be reason to believe that man was an unchangeable being, and that, therefore, any attempts to make him either better or worse must be nugatory. As, however, such a uniformity does not exist—as some men are ignorant and others wise, some vicious and others virtuous, and even the same individual, at times, undergoes a change in almost all his feelings and convictions and actions—we cannot but conclude that character, whether good or bad, is nothing more than a factitious quality acquired by man—an impression, as it were, made by surrounding circumstances upon that which constitutes human existence—and that it is dependent upon the particular organization of every individual, in connection with the particular occurrences or circumstances by which that organization has been surrounded and influenced. The material compound of the European and the Ethiopian are alike, and yet the two are different in colour, in creed, and in extent of knowledge and refinement. Opposed as they are, however, the two races might be made to change characters and opinions, simply by subjecting each to those specific influences which have heretofore operated upon the other. In like manner may all human beings, by exposure to the operation of certain circumstances and influences, be made savage or civilized, ignorant or enlightened, immoral or religious. That such will be and ever is the case, is a fact indisputably proved by the testimony of all history, and the daily experience of men.

Such, then, being the nature of man, and such the influence of circumstances upon him, his destiny is placed within his own hands; and it is in the power of society, as a whole, to determine, by the establishment of particular social institutions, what shall be the general character and habits of its individual members. Thus the evils of every kind now endured may not only be alleviated, but totally removed.

Everything which in any way operates upon or influences man is a circumstance. Men perform no action without a motive of some kind; and all their motives to thought and to exertion arise, either immediately or remotely, from the operation of surrounding circumstances upon them. If deprived of food, men become hungry—if of drink, thirsty—if disappointed in their expectations and thwarted in their desires, they are discontented and unhappy. All these feelings or sensations are the effects of particular circumstances upon sentient organization—they cannot be destroyed by any mere effort of thinking or willing—and thus they become the causes of motives and the inciters to action. From the nature of man, therefore, he must ever be the creature of circumstances—he will ever passively receive impressions from surrounding objects— for he cannot, by taking thought, alter his organization, or make it independent of external influences, or add one cubit to his stature.

But, although passive as to the manner in which he will receive an impression from a particular circumstance, man may acquire a power of determining whether or not he will expose himself to the influence of such circumstance. He is passive in reference to the present, but active as regards the future. It has always been the end of man's endeavours to control, in some degree, the circumstances which made him happy or miserable. To this end, he has never, by reasoning upon the matter, tried to prevent him-self from being hungry or thirsty, but he has endeavoured to keep a supply of food and drink always at hand. The hunger controls the man, and the food, in turn, controls the hunger; and if the food be not forthcoming, the man will die. Thus, while the hunger is master of the man, the man himself, by having food in his possession, is master of the hunger, and therefore master of his own life, or of this one circumstance which affects his life. Man is always thus alternately a passive and an active being—operated upon and operating—but every desire which he feels, and every action which he performs, result from the combined action and reaction of circumstance and organization upon each other.

In respect to character, man has a capacity to be any-thing, and by turns everything, as circumstances shall determine. He, like the floating bubble on the stream, shews us, at times, many colours and mixtures of colours; but these various shades of character, however light or dark, are little more than reflex radiations from surround-ing objects and occurrences. The simple nature of man is colourless—it is fitted to receive every variety of impres-sion—and, when the combined nature and impression call forth an action, good or bad, such action discloses not so much the hue of the nature itself, as the hue which it has taken from the bright or the gloomy influences to which it has been exposed. Man cannot, therefore, be justly blamed or hated by his fellows for being what the circum-stances and influences of his life have made him—whether a bloodthirsty tyrant, or a grasping capitalist, or a crouch-ing slave. If we would have the family of man to be, as it were, a bright and glorious assemblage of the pictures of humanity, we must place all men in positions and surround them with circumstances and influences in which there is nothing black and unseemly. It matters not what may be the mere knowledge given to men, or the moral precepts taught to them, if the circumstances by which they are surrounded be disregarded. Bad circumstances and influences can neither produce nor maintain good men. Circumstances furnish the seed of good or ill, and man is but as the soil in which they grow—the characters of men may be made entirely good, or entirely bad, or, as now, a variegated mixture of good and bad; but if the institutional circumstances and influences which surround man do not accord with the end desired—do not contain within them more of good than of evil—that which was intended to be a beautiful garden will become either choked up with noxious weeds, or converted into a blighted and barren waste.

All these considerations respecting the nature of man, and the influence of surrounding circumstances upon that nature, plainly show that the present habits and prejudices of the various classes of society, and their feelings of reverence or contempt towards each other, result from the social position of one class with respect to another, and the difference of the circumstances by which each class is surrounded; and, therefore, it necessarily follows—what has been proved by universal experience—that were the position and circumstances of each class reversed, the characters of each would be changed, and the crawling slave of to-day would become the domineering tyrant of to-morrow. All men are of one substance and one nature—they are made into tyrants and slaves by the present social system — by the division of society into rich and poor ; and this division is maintained, not because the first class is superior to the last in mental and corporeal attributes, but because the two exchange unequally with each other.

History shews us how little has been the success of man in controlling the various circumstances which have relation to his existence and his happiness. Wofully has he sinned and suffered. He has blindly destroyed the wealth and shed the blood of his fellow-man, simply because his fellow-man felt and thought just the same as he himself would have felt and thought, had he been placed the same position and exposed to the same influences. The tyranny and wrong at any to be removed, is not in the

men, but in the institutions; and wherever a physical
revolution has overturned a governmental despotism, and
left untouched the social institutions from which that despotism sprang, it has never led, and never can lead, to
any other result than a transfer of power from one man or
one class to another; for the last are left exposed to the
same influences as the first, and therefore they necessarily
revive the apparently subverted tyranny. Governmental
despotism and tyranny of every kind can be effectually
annihilated only by destroying the cause of such tyranny
—the empire of love can be extended from families and
friends to nations and the world at large, only by uprooting those social institutions which circumscribe the love
of man to man within the narrow circle of a class—and
all this can be done only by instituting arrangements based
on the broad principle of equality of rights.

Thus, then, the highest and most mighty performance
which man can achieve, will be to call into being and direct those social circumstances which control and influence
himself. From his very nature, man cannot resist the
operation of circumstances when they are once let loose
upon him—it is a condition of his being to yield to them,
and to derive from them his feelings and motives to action.
How almost omnipotent, then, will become the power of
man, when he can himself direct the circumstances which
he is compelled to obey—when he can, as it were, hold
both good and evil in his right hand! This power over
his own destiny may be obtained by man, and will one day
be exerted by him, through the instrumentality of his
social institutions. All his former achievements—his
conquests over the elements and forces of nature—are but
as so many steps towards an end yet to be attained. The
world is in its nonage rather than its dotage; and that
which has been already accomplished by man will fall as
far short of what he may do, as the efforts of boyhood
dwindle into insignificance when compared with the performances of maturity.

The various controllable circumstances which have
relation to the happiness of man, may be divided into
physical and moral,—or, such as are connected with the
production of wealth for the satisfaction of his animal
wants, and those which have reference to his intellectual
and moral cultivation, and his duty to his fellows. The

present social system furnishes abundant examples of both
the effective and defective means adopted to control
the first order of circumstances ; and, knowing exactly
what is wanted—the greatest quantity of wealth for
the least portion of labour—there can be no difficulty in selecting those modes of action which most
materially conduce to the end desired. In regard to the
attainment of a high degree of moral and intellectual
power, there are, under the present system, neither institutions nor arrangements favourable to the government of
this order of circumstances. Everything is defective, and
incapable of imbuing men with those qualities and feelings
which are so indispensable to their true happiness. Every
man is placed in a social position which utterly prevents
him from doing to all men as he would that all men should
do unto him. The divisions of society which now exist,
leave one class at the mercy of another, and make the gain
of the oppressor flow from the losses of the oppressed ; and
thus they necessarily make men enemies. These gradations, moreover, inflict on the great mass of the community
excessive toil and anxiety to procure the means of
subsistence ; and that desire for intellectual improvement
which is not destroyed by such toil and anxiety, withers
and dies in the cheerless atmosphere of poverty. Thus,
under the present system, there can be no such thing as
general morality—no such thing as the general cultivation
of the intellectual powers—and no possibility of men
being united together in that common bond of social love
which is so requisite to human progression.

Under the present system, every transaction relating to
the production and distribution of wealth is more or less
governed by the ever-active and ever-warring principle of
competition. It is perpetually bringing individuals and
classes into hostile collision with each other. Its province
is, not to determine what is right, but what is expedient.
Under its guidance, the interests of men are individualised,
and separated from each other ; and every one is left at
liberty to advance his own particular welfare, without any
reference to the interests and the welfare of those with
whom he may come in contact.

In connection with competition, and working with it in
the production of wealth, is co-operation. Every work of
nature and of art affords evidence of the power of co-ope-

ration, or the union and direction of forces. The stately tree of the forest and the massive mansion of the city, alike owe their existence to co-operation. Without this principle, there could exist neither civilization nor refinement, for the whole time of every individual would be occupied in isolated endeavours to obtain subsistence. Every one would be poor and miserable, and all the results of labour would be unsatisfactory and unremunerative. By well-directed co-operation, however, there is nothing accomplishable which may not be effected. The power of any nation or community will ever be in proportion to the co-operation which exists among its members ; but all the powers and advantages of co-operation cannot be fully developed and enjoyed, unless there be among men a perfect union of interests and reciprocity of benefits ; and there can be no such union and reciprocity except labour be universal and exchanges equal.

Competition is a consequence arising from the operation of surrounding circumstances and influences upon human organization. It is set in motion by the uncontrolled self-love of man ; and it can be destroyed only by subjecting men to a peculiar course of moral training, or by creating for all persons a sufficiency of the articles desired and competed for. Either of these means will be destructive of competition ; for the first will supplant it by higher feelings and actions, while under the last it can have no scope for exertion. But under the present social system, and the feelings and modes of action which this system calls into existence, the spirit of competition is an ineradicable and an indestructible ingredient in human character ; for wherever two or more parties are actuated by similar desires for particular objects, they will compete with each other for possession, so long as competition is the only means by which these objects can be obtained.

Competition is only one of a class of human feelings and actions which originate from uncontrolled self-love, and which ever produce discord, envy, hatred, and all uncharitableness. It should be recollected that man, whether in civilized or savage society, comes into the world a human being in the rough, and brings with him all the instincts and feelings appertaining to a state of brute existence. These are what have been implanted in man for his preservation—they are the animal part of humanity—the involuntary movements of the principle of existence to hold fast to being. But those unregulated instincts and actions which would tend to the preservation and enjoyment of man if he were alone in the world, become absolutely prejudicial to him if thus left uncontrolled in a state of society. These instincts and faculties operate just as strongly upon man in society, as they would do if he were isolated ; but society is an artificial state of existence—an appliance of human reason to rear a superstructure, of which the foundation only has been laid by Nature—and therefore man's natural incentives to action must be artificially constrained and guided, that they may conduce to, instead of thwarting, the great design of society. Unless thus controlled, there cannot be that universal happiness which must have existence before there can be any true individual happiness : for the last, when rightly viewed, is no more than a reflection from the first.

Thus, instead of vainly endeavouring to eradicate the principle of self-love, institutions must be established which will govern and direct this principle, and compel it to benefit society at large, at the same time that it benefits the individual in whom it operates. This can be done only by means of institutions in which individuality, as such, is unknown—in which the man is lost in the mass—in which all interests and benefits are as one.

We have, then, the true principles on which to base a social system—we possess, likewise, sufficient knowledge of the nature and capabilities of the being for whom this system is intended—we have, also, an abundant accumulation of facts connected with the effective and defective modes of acting upon these principles, as well as of the particular effects produced upon man by all these varieties of action—and it can therefore be determined, with certainty, what will be the character and worldly condition of individuals and nations when subjected to the influence of institutions founded on a wise application of these principles.

The consideration of what is essential to a proper social system is widely different from the subversion of an existing system and the establishment of the one desired. Men are so influenced by custom, that, although they may be shewn the end of a great movement, and the immense advantages derivable from it, they will rarely attempt to

travel towards the desired object, unless it happen to lie
directly in their way, and can be attained with little difficulty.   The very idea of change, however bright the prospect held out, terrifies the great majority of individuals, if
such change happen to lead them out of the common
beaten track of every-day existence.   They are ever ready
to convert molehills into mountains, and to regard as an
insurmountable obstacle that which is scarcely sufficient to
make them stumble.   In considering, then, how a social
change is to be effected, a survey must be taken not only of
the end itself, bnt likewise of the various means by which
such end may be attained, and the efficiency of the means
already possessed by those who desire the change; that the
enterprise fail not from inadequate and injudicious measures on the one hand, nor despair of its accomplishment
on the other.

CHAPTER IX.

THE DIFFICULTIES ATTENDANT ON A CHANGE OF SYSTEM.

It cannot be doubted that the duration of society, or the communion of human beings with each other, will be as lengthened as the existence of man; and that a social system may be devised and established, containing the requisites considered, and productive of the good effects desired, is apparent even from so much of the nature and power of man as the present system brings into view.

Society is now, in every nation, split up into small knots or assemblages of persons, more or less isolated in respect to the world at large; and these divisions are termed families. To one of these minor portions does every individual belong; it is to him a world in miniature, and in its narrow sphere is centred and confined his best and warmest feelings. In families there is a bond of sympathy, a community of interest and of feeling, which does not embrace society as a whole. By analysing these family feelings and attractions, however, and examining attentively their growth, and the cause of their continuance and decay, it has been concluded that they owe their force more to their incessant exercise and the circumscribed sphere of their action, than to any peculiar tie connected with relationship; and that, therefore, if there be instituted particular social arrangements, which shall enlarge, as it were, the relationship of every individual from family to kind, the same feelings and sympathies may be extended throughout society, and all mankind " live in the equal brotherhood of love." It requires no arguments to prove that the world at large will be much wealthier, much wiser, and therefore much happier, than it is at the present moment or has been at any former time, when the sympathies and interests of all mankind are as one. But there can be no such union except where labour is universal and its produce equally enjoyed,—where each individual is exposed to similar and only to good influences,—and where each member of society is shewn and made to see and feel that his true interest is to be found only in the interest of every other member of the community.

The present separation of society into jarring and hostile sections is irremediable under the existing system; for the continuance of such separation and hostility is insured by the sole circumstance of there being among men a diversity of interests, which, operating in contrary ways, necessarily bring men into collision with each other, because they make the gain of one man to be the loss of another. It is now, even apart from relationship, the interest of a son that his parent should gain wealth, for he expects thereby that he will be better provided for—it is the interest of a parent that his children should acquire property, that they may be able to succour him in his old age—it is the interest of relatives that each other should possess enough and to spare, that any one of them, if unfortunate, may obtain assistance; but experience proves, in thousands of instances, that the ties of blood cannot unite those whom interest separates.

Under the present system there is not, and there never can be, a general community of interest, for the interest of every class is opposed to the interest of every other class; and nothing can be gained by the capitalist which is not lost by the producer. It is not now the interest of the working man that the capitalist or employer should obtain greater profits, because the profits thus obtained by the last are the accumulated losses of the first; nor is it the interest of the capitalist that the working man should receive the full fruits of his labour, because, were such the case, the capitalist could not hold supremacy, and live in idleness and luxury, as he now does. The assertion, that if the employer obtain great profits he will be enabled to pay high wages, is a fallacy which daily contradicts itself. As the capitalist becomes more wealthy, he increases his expenditure, or invests more capital. Where his profits rise from £200 to £400 or £800 per annum, no corresponding rise, and no rise whatever, takes place in the wages of his workmen. The old rate of payment is maintained through all these advances; but when a reverse takes place, and profits decrease, the first thing thought of by an employer, is,—not whether he shall retrench his expenditure, and forego some of his luxuries, and come down to his original standard, but *how much he shall reduce the wages of his workmen ;* for his own station, and pride, and pomp, must remain untouched. Thus the division of society into classes perpetuates the division of interests ; and, by bringing individuals into hostile contact in the common scramble for subsistence, destroys those germs of sympathy and good feeling which naturally exist in all men. Under present arrangements, each division of society is systematically trained to believe itself superior or inferior to other divisions—each is systematically trained to believe that its interests are more or less advanced by the depression of other interests—and each imbibes feelings and prejudices differing from the others, and applicable to its own position on the social map. Thus is society—thus do men think, act, and feel.

Whatever may be the alterations made, it is certain that a worse system than the present one can by no possibility be devised ; and it would be equally impossible to make a social change of any kind, which would leave society in as bad a state as it now is. Such being the case, and there being abundant proof that man can be trained to imbibe good or bad feelings towards his fellows—to dwell with them in equality, or rule as king, or obey as subject—it has been conceived that, by instituting a social system which shall do away with the present gradations in society, and unite all the individuals of a nation into one great family, where good offices shall be reciprocal, and all interests one and indivisible, there can exist only feelings akin to those now felt in isolated families. It has long been seen that a diversity of interests must always be destructive of social harmony, because necessarily subversive of those feelings of individual attachment and respect which form the only basis on which universal love and peace can be reared. In order, therefore, to reconcile those interests which are now opposed, by uniting all into one interest, and to extend universally that love which is now pent up within the narrow circle of a family, a system has been attempted to be established, in which labour shall be universal, in which the land and all productive property shall be held and enjoyed in common, and in which rights and duties shall be as equal as the capabilities of man under the best circumstances will admit of. In this improved system, there can be, from the nature of the principles on which it is founded, neither rich nor poor, neither employers nor employed, in the present sense of the terms ; but a general equality of condition and of political power will prevail universally. Instead of people residing in unhealthy and incommodious dwellings and towns, like those at present existing, society will be divided into an indefinite number of communities or families, comprising from 1,000 to 5,000 individuals, who will dwell and labour in extensive and well-devised buildings, and create and enjoy every necessary and luxury in the greatest abundance. All persons will be educated and trained in the best manner that knowledge and experience can devise. The present forms of government, with the wars and crimes and follies existing in perpetual and indissoluble connection with them, will be unknown ; and the terrors and wrongs alike of despotism and anarchy will be feared and suffered no longer. A pure and rational liberty will be universally enjoyed ; and every man will do as he would be done by, and love his neighbour as himself. Thus situated—thus controlling the good and the bad circumstances which surround them, and operated upon by none of the vile and paltry feelings which more or less now influence all men—the physical, moral, and intellectual character of every individual will attain the highest standard of human excellence, and all the present evils and vices of society will be entirely removed.

Based on the great principle of human equality of rights, the social system of community of possessions will work out its results by means of the following arrangements :—

1. Arrangements for the production and equable distribution of an unlimited quantity of wealth.

2. Arrangements for the physical, moral, and intellectual culture of every member of society.

3. Arrangements for the proper government of society at large.

Under these three general heads may be included everything relating to man and his institutions. They embrace all things that have relation to his existence and his happiness. They are even now more or less kept in view by all nations, for they cannot be lost sight of in any social system whatever.

The first class of arrangements relates to the erection of buildings for domestic, manufacturing, and commercial purposes, in which shall be combined all that can conduce to the preservation of health, and to production; the creation and distribution of food and all other kinds of produce, the construction of roads, railways, canals, and all the various requisites to unlimited production and speedy distribution.

Under the second head are comprised such arrangements as relate to education, in the fullest sense of the term; to the formation of character upon the best principles and from the best models known—the practice as well as the knowledge of morality and charity—the love of truth, and virtue, and social harmony—the establishment of institutions for relaxation and amusement—and all other regulations having relation to social rights and duties, and the proper development and direction of the powers of body and mind.

To the third class belong such arrangements as are necessary to the proper regulation and government of society;—in regard to the devising and instituting of the best means for the production and distribution of wealth; the adjustment of production and consumption throughout society at large, as well as the commercial relations with foreign countries; the education and training of individuals, and the settlement of differences, and the protection of children and invalids; and the devising and establishing of all other regulations having reference to the control of production and distribution, and the protection of persons and property.

When thus founded, and containing in perfection all these arrangements, there can be no doubt that such a system would, from its very nature, accomplish all that it is possible for the powers of man to achieve.

In the system itself, as well as in the arrangements, there is nothing which has not been more or less acted upon by man since his creation; and nothing which is incompatible with, or destructive of, the most perfect equality of rights. There is merely an extension and classification—not a creation—of principles. The com-

mon feelings and attachments of human nature will be
neither destroyed nor weakened, but strengthened and
expanded until they embrace nations as well as individuals
and families.   The production and distribution of wealth
will not cease, and poverty and desolation overspread the
land, but the most potent powers which human ingenuity
can conquer will be made to produce wealth of every kind,
in quantities limited only by the desires of man.   The
peace of society will not be perpetually invaded, and men
left to prey upon and slaughter each other, as is now the
case, but a universal love and harmony will exist throughout society, for all the causes of discord will be annihilated.   Governmental despotism and irresponsible authority
will not, as they now do, seize upon the produce of
industry and rule men with a rod of iron, but there will
exist a universal freedom, founded on the most perfect
equality of rights, and held in subjection by the best of
all possible governments—self-government.   There will be
neither tyranny, nor slavery, nor crime, for the incentives
to these things will no longer have existence.   There will
be no possibility of childhood remaining unprotected or
old age unprovided for ; and thus the young and the old
will be no longer tortured with those dark visions of the
future, which now palsy the better feelings of so many
hearts, and embitter the few allotted hours of man's existence.   All these things, and all else that are attainable,
can be possessed and enjoyed by mankind only under a
social system where labour is universal, where land and
capital are held in common, and where equal rights and
equal laws will be enjoyed in the fullest extent.

In contrast with such a state of things, what does the
present system offer ?   Even in its best and brightest parts
how much is there wanting—in the purest and most unal-
loyed emanations of charity and love to which it can give
birth, how cold, and vitiated, and unexpanded is every
feeling !   In the existing arrangements for the creation
and distribution of wealth, every thing is defective and
unjust.   An inadequate quantity is produced, and the
greater part of this limited portion is enjoyed or wasted by
those who have done little, and those who have done
nothing, towards its creation.   For the working man there
is no real enjoyment, either present or prospective ; but his
life's horizon is bounded by the well-known land-marks of

unpitied poverty and unassisted decrepitude. View the present system as we will—either in respect to the creation and enjoyment of wealth continually and universally, the certain and adequate provision for all accidents and contingencies, the growth and the practice of the higher virtues, the advancement of the arts and sciences, and the facilities afforded for the attainment of individual or universal happiness—there is nothing in this system which can be regarded as a sufficient recommendation for its continuance. Every good which is now enjoyed can be likewise enjoyed under a system of community of possessions and equality of condition; while all those evils which flow from the present arrangements of society will be entirely escaped from, and be felt and known no longer.

The political economists and capitalists have made many objections to the social system of community of possessions and equality of rights; and have advanced many arguments to shew that the system cannot be established, or, if momentarily set to work, can never be permanently acted upon. Some of their reasons are intended to prove that the productive classes—the persons most interested in the contemplated change—can never accumulate sufficient money to commence the new system, by the purchase of the fixed capital of the country from those who now hold it; that they will never be able to prevail upon the capitalists to assist them in the enterprise; that if isolated communities be established, they will ultimately fail from the immorality or general bad habits of the parties comprising them; and that, even if the new system were partially commenced in despite of all these obstacles, the communities would fail from the inability of their members to compete in production with that part of society remaining under the present system.

The weight of these objections can be determined only by an impartial survey of all the means which may be made available in forwarding the contemplated change, and completing it after it has been commenced. To accomplish the change, and free Labour from the dominion of Capital, it is necessary that the land and reproducible wealth of the country should be in possession of the working class. Their endeavours, therefore, have been chiefly directed to the accumulation of a sum of money sufficiently large to enable a certain number of persons to

purchase the land and fixed capital of the country from
those who now possess it, that the new arrangements
might be immediately commenced by the formation of at
least one social community. Partly, however, from the
general ignorance which prevails respecting the end
desired, and partly from the hostility of those classes
interested in maintaining the present supremacy of Capital
over Labour, in no case has a sufficient fund been accumulated to afford a community any chance of success. Distrust and division, also, have at times put a premature end
to these struggles, and the undertaking has ended in con-
tention and confusion.

The productive classes, from their present position in
society, are necessarily poor ; and therefore most of their
endeavours to benefit themselves have been, in a great
degree, cramped and damned at the very outset. There
are, besides, vast masses of workmen in a state of such
abject poverty—and poverty, too, daily extending in its
operation and increasing in its intensity—that the accumulations of whole generations of them would advance
but little the establishment of the system of community.
But, notwithstanding all these disadvantages, there are
sufficient funds at this moment in the hands of the various operative Benefit Societies in the United Kingdom to
establish several communities directly. The late trades'
unions, also, afford evidence of the power of the working
classes, poor as they are, to raise vast sums of money ; and
although these sums sink into insignificance when considered as the means by which a social system is to be at
once subverted, they are quite adequate to the *commencement* of common-stock institutions. Thus, it is evident
that it is in the power of the working classes, as a body, to
set the new system in motion by their own unaided endeavours—by the trifling subscription of even one penny per
week—and when once fairly established, it would under-
mine the present system in all directions, and bring it
down in ruins.

In addition to the power thus inherently possessed by
the producers, there have at times been found, and there
are yet existing, wealthy capitalists willing to assist in the
glorious work of human emancipation from poverty and
vice. By the aid of a number of such individuals, common-stock communities might be established, and ulti-

mately work out the end desired. It may be said, that,
by the aid of such capitalists, a community was once partially established—that an approximation was made to
universal labour and equal exchanges, because all the
members of the community were to assist in production,
and then enjoy in common the wealth produced—that
buildings were erected, and the various members set to
work—and that, in a short time, the attempt completely
failed, the community was dissolved into its primitive
elements, and the land and buildings were sold and applied
to other purposes. But in this partial attempt, made without due consideration of the obstacles to be surmounted,
the wealth invested was of very limited amount, and totally
inadequate to meet the exigencies of the case ; and this
cause alone was sufficient to ensure failure. Thus confined
in their endeavours at the very beginning, and dispirited
by the slow progress of the system, and the many difficulties and annoyances to which their want of means and
their isolated position exposed them, the capitalists and
others engaged in the enterprise ultimately withdrew their
assistance from an attempt which appeared to promise so
unfavourably.

But it is likewise objected by the economists—and the
preceding example is brought forward as proof—that, even
had there been adequate funds, the general habits of society at large are incompatible with the existence of any
other than the present social system—that man, with his
present class and caste education and prejudices, could not
go at once into a social system of community, and dwell
in harmony and equality with his fellows. All these arguments, however, are drawn from a consideration of man *as
he is at present*—without reference to the causes which
have made him thus, and without any consideration as to
whether these causes may not be supplanted by others, and
other effects be thereby produced. Therefore all such
objections go no further than to point out the difficulties
attendant on the first establishment of the system of community.

Human nature is human nature throughout the whole
world ; but its manifestations are as various and contradictory as are the colours, creeds, and languages of men.
All mankind are possessed of the like faculties, propensities, and qualities of being, and yet no two individuals,

think, feel, or act precisely the same ; nor are the thoughts, feelings, and actions of the same person invariable and unalterable. Thus, while it is confessed that there is not now amongst men that intellectuality, that charity, that high sense of honour, that genuine morality, which is essential to the proper working of a system of equality,— it cannot be denied that, by intermediate arrangements, individuals may be sufficiently imbued with these requisite qualities to commence the change.

Instead of tracing these miscarriages to their proper cause, the capitalists and economists have at once set them down as the natural and inevitable results of every attempt to subvert the present system and establish the principles of equality. They hold them up as beacons to warn the discontented and the charitable of the hopelessness of their condition and the futility of their endeavours. But these failures to establish universal labour and equal remuneration have arisen from particular circumstances, well ascertained and remediable ; and such momentary ill-successes can no more be regarded as proofs of the impossibility of establishing and acting upon the system of equality, than can the slow progress of science in the early ages be considered as indicative of the chimerical and worthless character of its great truths. There have never yet been sufficient means — either monetary or moral—devoted to the establishment of the new system, to afford a well-grounded hope of success. To the causes of failure arising from insufficient funds, must be added those causes dependent on the parties who attempted the change. The individuals who entered the projected common-stock community were taken almost promiscuously from the world at large, and they carried with them their old feelings, prejudices, and habits,—all of which were incompatible with the existence of any kind of equality, because, being part and parcel of the existing system, they were naturally subversive of any equality which might be established.

But, setting aside all these pecuniary difficulties, and those which relate to the moral character and amicable agreement of the communicants, it is contended by the economists, that the success of the new system is dependent on other causes than either change of character or the acquisition of a sufficient capital to commence effective proceedings ; and that, therefore, even if communities be established, they must very speedily fail. Taking society as they find it, with its multifarious divisions, its competition, and the redundancy and hopeless poverty of the labouring classes, the economists maintain that those persons in a community, although labouring universally and enjoying in common, will be no better off in respect to all the comforts and luxuries of life, than those who remain under the present system. Reasoning thus, they say :—A community must produce within itself every article of which it is in want, or it must produce a commodity which it can exchange for the article desired. It is intended that the labour of those in community shall not much exceed the half of the labour performed by the workers in the present system : if there be less labour there will be proportionately less wealth created, and therefore less to consume, and less to exchange for the articles wanted ; consequently, commodities will be nearly twice as dear in community as they are out—or in other words, when trading with the world at large, those in community will receive only half as much of a commodity, in exchange for the proceeds of their labour of six hours a day, as those who are not in community will receive for their twelve hours. If all the wealth that is obtained in community be equally enjoyed, such equality in distribution will be no recompense for the insufficient quantity received ; and if the people work long hours, and produce more, their situa_ tion will then, upon the whole, be little better than that of those remaining under the old system. In respect to trading matters, it is not possible that the individual who works in community about six hours a day, should com_ pete with the half-starved labourer who toils twelve hours per day under the present system ; for, let the staple produce of a community be what it may—let any and every kind of machinery be employed—the same staple will be produced by the same machinery in old society, and will always be cheaper in the last than in the first Taxes, also, and rents, will be paid, directly or indirectly. by those in community as well as by those out of it : and they will likewise be equally subject to all those rates and imposts which come under the denomination of govern_ mental burthens.   A community would thus stand some_ what in the character of a small farming and manufac_ turing establishment ; and it is well known that the

majority of small farmers and manufacturers can barely
make ends meet, even when they are proprietors, unless
subjected to constant labour and anxiety.

The whole of these objections of the economists—fatal
as they appear when levelled against an isolated community in a country such as Great Britain, and surrounded,
as such community would be, by hostile interests of every
description—are powerless when applied to the system of
community of possessions *as a system*. A whole and a
part are not synonymous terms ; and, in the present case,
the objections applied to the one do not in the least affect
the other. Society, in the same manner as are the individuals of which it is composed, is and always will be made
up of many parts, each performing its specified duties, and
each part indispensable to the well-being of the whole.
There must always be arrangements for the production and
distribution of food and necessaries, and also for the intellectual and moral cultivation of society at large, as well as
for the government and guidance of its members. It will
happen in every country, that, while one part is favourable
to the production of food, another portion will be better
adapted to the manufacture of hardware, or pottery, or
cloth ; and upon the judicious management of these advantages will depend the greater or less saving in the labour
and time devoted to the production of wealth. The
various difficulties of this nature, therefore, which stand in
the way of the success of an isolated community, can have
no existence in a *system of communities*.

Besides, in comparing the relative position of parties in
and out of community, the economists assume that those
in a community will, by the present arrangements of
society, be compelled to contribute to the support of the
unproductive classes not in the community. They thus
take away the very essence and spirit of the system of
community—its great distinguishing features of universal
labour and equal exchanges—and the system of community
becomes, in their hands, a mere modification of the present
system, and suffering all the burthens and wrongs endured
under the existing system. The entire removal of all
these social and governmental imposts is one great characteristic of the system of community of possessions and
equality of rights ; for, as a system, it will be destructive
of all such grievances. The little expense incurred by

government will be in the prevention instead of the punishment of crime, and the prevention instead of the prosecution of war against neighbouring states; for, under the present system, the protection of persons and property, the carrying on of wars, and the payment of debts arising out of such wars, form the chief items in governmental expenditure.

These things, and the institutions connected with them, are indissolubly bound up with the existing system; and may be regarded as the chief flood-gates through which the greedy shoals of civil, ecclesiastical, and military vampires are let in upon a people.

Thus, as a system, community of possessions will do for a nation those things which, with the present system, cannot be done under any circumstances; and it would be just as rational to point to the severed head and limbs of a man, as evidences of his powerlessness, as it is to judge of the results of the system of community by the feeble operations of an isolated portion of it.

Community of possessions is in every respect the most perfect form of society which man can institute, and it therefore requires a corresponding degree of excellence in the character and qualities of all who enjoy its influence. That modification of the principle of community and equality already considered, which unites society at large into one great family, where there is nothing but harmony and love, is the last remove which man can make towards perfection. It may be said, therefore, that we might as well expect to behold the fly to spring up at once from the maggot, as expect that man can go, by one remove, from the present system into one so dissimilar in all its parts as is the system of community. The worm which is taken from amidst putrescency will defile all that it touches, and stink wherever it may be placed,—and yet it contains in embryo the plumed and gaudy insect which is to sport in the sunbeam and dance upon the breeze. It is time and circumstance which bring about the change: by successive steps does the transformation progress, and the last remove completes the work.

So, likewise, must it be with man. The foul and loathsome selfishness which now more or less accompanies every action, clings to every thought, and pollutes every aspiration, is part of the system in which man has for so

many ages moved.   Daily experience proves that the present social system is altogether unfavourable to the attainment of a high standard of excellence in regard to
character—that its customs, and modes of action throughout, tend only to generate corrupt feelings and bad practices, and to bring into play the lowest and the worst of
man's faculties.   Every step to the establishment of a
better system must be made by those who have grown up
under the present system, and who are, therefore, more or
less imbued with the depravity and ill-feelings which this
system generates.   A mere knowledge of the principles of
equality is not the only requisite for the establishment of
community of possessions.   There must likewise exist the
requisite feelings and moral qualities, all well developed,
and accompanied by high intellectual powers.   If, then, a
changed character be essential to the success of the social
system of community in its most perfect form—and if,
likewise, the present system affords no circumstances and
no facilities for effecting the requisite change of character,
and preparing man for the higher and better state desired
—it is evident that things must necessarily remain as they
are, unless one of two methods be adopted.   Either those
who commence the new system must be possessed of
accumulations of capital sufficient to overcome the draw-
backs of every kind imposed by the present system, until
the superior circumstances created by the new system shall
have done their work, and generated a race of human
beings widely different in character and habits from those
who now exist;—or else some preparatory step must be
discovered and made use of—some movement partaking
partly of the present and partly of the desired system—
some intermediate resting-place, to which society may go
with all its faults and all its follies, and from which it may
move forward, imbued with those qualities and attributes
without which the system of community and equality cannot as such have existence.

When once fairly set in motion, a new social system
must, from the operation of a law of nature constant and
invariable, generate men and modes of action in accordance
with its own nature and protective of its own existence.
There is in all things a faculty of action and reaction,
which, did no extraneous interferences occur, would prevent all other changes, and stamp with perpetuity things

as they are, or were. This predisposition to continuance is no more than a modification of that immutable law by which like causes would be compelled to produce like effects. But causes are not, and never can be, precisely alike, and therefore effects are never exactly the same. To be a like cause, one cause must operate at the same time, in the same place, upon the same things, in the same manner, and under all the circumstances in which some other cause is acting—the supposition of which is absurd and incomprehensible. Thus, although it is the nature of the present social system to generate characters and institutions in agreement with itself, and protective of itself, the common aberration of causation is slowly but irresistibly progressing, and generating in its course new forces and new organic disturbances, which must inevitably bring on decline, and dissolution, and recomposition. Thus rise and fall all systems—thus are created and destroyed all beings—thus are framed and subverted all institutions.

With regard to the institution of the social system of community of possessions and equality of rights, it is possible, from the nature of the change, and from a consideration of what has at times been done by them, that it may ultimately be accomplished even by the unaided endeavours and small savings of the working classes; and that it might, also, in course of time, be effected by the partial union of the capitalists with the producers; and this, too, without political or social disturbances, or any immediately perceptible effect upon the existing laws and arrangemente of society at large. But the experience of all times goes to shew, that no enterprise can be regarded as secure of accomplishment, if it depend for success on the self-denial of masses of people, who, living almost from hand to mouth on the produce of their labour, and harassed by the perpetual calls of a family for subsistence, are made by their position the slaves of the moment, and are incapacitated from taking much from the present to provide against the future. The capitalists and economists are perpetually advising the productive classes to live abstemiously, and hoard up every trifle which can be screwed from their stomachs or their backs; but such counsel, however good it may be, never can be acted upon to any great extent, for it is not in human nature to go on until death like a mere machine, if there be allied with it any degree of feeling or intellectuality beyond that of a beast of burthen. Make men susceptible of enjoyment, either animal or intellectual, and that will they seek for and obtain, despite of consequences ; and so long as a poor class is surrounded by the example of a rich class, and exposed to every temptation which depraved ingenuity can invent to excite and gratify factitious wants, it is in vain to hope that the allurements of the senses can be withstood, unless there be created motives more powerful than those arising from the mere chance of enjoying a better social position at some remote period. Desultory and isolated endeavours of mere fractions of society, likewise, from their very nature, are much more likely to fail than to succeed ; and that such efforts can be little else than desultory and isolated, is apparent from the fact, that a vast and progressively increasing portion of society, from their position and the dearth of means at their disposal, are so inextricably bound up with the present system, that only a general movement of the community at large can effect their deliverance.

That no means of effecting the desired change may be wanting, we will now consider another plan of operations—which, while it contains all the essentials of the modes already reviewed, is free from their defects, in respect to the time in which the change may be accomplished, the numbers who will be at once included in its benefits, and the facilities which it affords for taking society just as it is, without material alteration either in human character, or domestic arrangements, or the existing modes of creating or distributing wealth.

As a first step to the consideration of such an intermediate social change, we will examine into the nature and operation of that first great element of the power of the capitalist—Money. Such a review, while it will tend to enforce yet stronger upon the working class the necessity of a change of system, will at the same time acquaint them with the secret of the almost omnipotent might of the capitalist ; and enable them to perceive how easily this power may be wrested from him, and made to subserve the great cause of human exaltation and happiness.

CHAPTER X.

THE NATURE AND USES OF MONEY.

From the general failure which has heretofore attended all political and social plans for ameliorating the condition of the working classes of the United Kingdom, the political economists, as is daily seen, have acquired increased faith in their own doctrines of inequality, and a more confirmed assurance that no other than their great remedy of restricting Labour to Capital can effect the object aimed at. We have seen that these men contemplate nothing more than what they conceive to be the improvement of the present system—that they would keep the whole human race divided into two classes—into rich and poor, or capitalists and producers—the one class wallowing in wealth, and the other placed just beyond "the verge of starvation." They do not expect that a man of the latter class should eat a meal until he has produced two—one for labour, and the other for "profit"—one for the workman, and the other for his employer, the capitalist. They would, therefore, have no more workers than could be "profitably employed" by the capitalists—or, in other words, they would limit the future increase of the working classes, and starve or transport to foreign countries all whom they, by the capital now in their possession, could not find employment for.

Such, it has been already shewn, is the remedy of the economists and capitalists; and that it may better work out its results, these men, with a cold-blooded and calculating "liberality," would remove all governmental restrictions regarding the hours of labour, the wages of workmen, and the trade to other nations. The state of society which would be induced by such a remedy as this,

may easily be conceived of; for it would present few features differing from the present. There would be, as
there now is, a high class and a low class—the former
enjoying the greater part of the wealth produced by the
incessant activity and toil of the latter.

It can only be considered that the economists and capitalists are actuated by the most insane stupidity, in supposing that such a systematically unjust division of
society as that which now exists, would be tolerated by
the working classes after its vileness and injustice had
been pointed out to them. Were men like steam-
engines formed to toil on, until dissolution, without feeling
and without thought—they might thus be methodically
worked to death, or starved, or expatriated ; but men are
intelligences—they have brains as well as bones and
sinews—and when they suffer wrongs, they look around
for remedies.

Knowing that labour was the source from whence arose
all capital—and seeing that the raw material of capital
was in abundance on every side, awaiting the power of
labour to produce the required transformation—it is
strange that the economists, when they stumbled upon
their remedy of *restricting population and labour to the
existing wants of capital,* never discovered the equally
obvious and far more natural and practicable plan of
*increasing capital in proportion to the growing wants of
population and labour.* A brief consideration of the
nature of capital will at once shew the practicability of
effecting this great object, and thereby do away with those
social evils which now directly arise from the disproportion
which apparently exists between capital and labour. It
is the present arrangements of society, and not any real
disproportion between population and the means of employment, which cause so many to pine in idleness, or to
sacrifice health in unremitting toil.

The review which has been taken of some of the attempts
made to subvert the present system, has shewn us that
these efforts have failed chiefly, if not entirely, from the
inadequate amount of money devoted to the purpose. As
money, then, is the one thing needful—the first thing
necessary to the success of every enterprise which has for
its object either the amendment of the present system or
the institution of a new one—what *is* money? What are

bank-notes and gold and silver coin? For these substances will men give up lands, houses, machinery, food, and all else that they have. Is money, then, as it were, the essence of these good things? Have certain portions of land, together with houses and food, been transformed, by the occult operations of some cunning alchymists, into slips of paper and pieces of metal? No; a change of this kind has not taken place; gold and silver are no more than simple metals, and bank-notes are but paper.

It would answer no purpose to enter at length into a consideration of the origin of money. It is evident that, before coin or bank-notes had existence, there must have been houses, food, and other kinds of wealth. Neither coin nor bank-notes can be eaten or inhabited: of themselves they are as worthless as the pebbles on the sea-shore. Some persons, then, must originally either have regarded the precious metals as commodities, or articles of barter, just the same as they did cattle and implements—or else they manufactured coin as a representative of these commodities, to assist them in their exchanges with each other. Gold and silver were regarded as commodities, and as intrinsic and real wealth, by the earliest and most polished nations. There is no evidence that the precious metals were ever considered by them *merely as representatives* of anything; such an idea does not appear to have been entertained prior to the introduction of paper money, which is a modern invention, and was originally created as a substitute for, or a representative of, gold and silver coin.

There is no subject upon which more general ignorance prevails among the productive classes, than on that of money. The great body of the people have no precise idea of what is meant by the term "money," nor do they ever reason upon the cause or the nature of its power. Many persons regard the words "Capital" and "Money" as having the same signification—capital meaning money, and money meaning capital; others separate the two, but consider that a certain quantity of gold or bank-notes is of the same intrinsic value, and that it therefore is just as much real capital, as a house or other article; others, regarding gold as equivalent to real property, separate from it the bank-notes, which they consider merely as the representatives of the gold, and as having, if separated from this foundation, no value whatever; while others, again, regard both gold and bank-notes merely as representatives of things produced, or fixed capital. But, notwithstanding the discrepancy of opinion and the confusion of ideas which prevail upon the subject, the man who is in possession of the sum of £10,000, either in gold or bank-notes, is considered by the world at large to be just as wealthy as he who is possessed of houses or machinery to the same amount; for it is well-known, that, by the custom of society, the gold and the bank-notes, inherently worthless as they may be, will procure for their holders either houses, food, or machinery, to the full amount of the nominal value of the gold or notes.

The political economists say that " Capital is hoarded labour"—" Capital is something produced with a view to further production;" and they divide capital into three kinds—into implements of labour, material on which labour is employed, and subsistence of labourers—the first being termed fixed capital, and the second and third reproducible capital. This definition and division altogether excludes gold, silver, and bank-notes; for it is evident, from the nature of these things, that they have no necessary connection with the real capital or wealth specified. Neither gold, silver, or notes can be regarded as implements of labour, material on which labour is employed, or subsistence of labourers. Thus money and capital, although often used as synonymous terms, are in themselves widely different: for money of every kind is, in reality, no more than a *representative of real capital*—a thing personifying or standing in the place of houses, implements, or food. It is solely on this account, and not from any inherent quality, that money is valuable; for by means of money, men are enabled, in greater or less portions, to make use of the real capital which they possess. Were there no such thing as money, the man who had a house, or any other valuable or bulky commodity, could make little or no use of it in the way of exchange: he could not give a part of it to the miller for some flour, and another part to the tailor for some clothes, for they would not trade upon a system involving such inextricable confusion among all parties. But this trouble and inconvenience is entirely removed by the invention of money; by means of which, whether gold or bank-notes, a man can as it were split up his house and other capital into innumerable fragments, and exchange or devour it piecemeal. From this mutual relation between capital and money, the two have become commonly identified, and money is universally regarded as equally valuable with real capital or existing produce ; but it is plain that money owes all its estimation to conventional usages, and that it is no more than an instrument for effecting exchanges.

Money is to capital, or real wealth, what the alphabet is to written language ; and as the latter consists merely of a number of arbitrary signs, signifying certain sounds, so in like manner do coin and bank-notes, in larger or smaller quantities, signify houses, or implements, or food, or anything else. The alphabets of all languages are sufficiently extensive to be made, by various combinations of the letters composing them, to express every variety of sound contained in these languages : the letters are neither too few nor too many. But in our monetary alphabet we have never yet followed this simple and natural plan of apportioning the means to the end. We have suffered it to remain deficient in every respect. Money, it it is true, has but one sound, and that sound signifies everything—*as far as it goes ;* but the money now in existence will no more represent *all* that should be thus personified, than can the letters *g o* be made to spell *good.* We may at present represent a horse, a house, a city, or a county—we might exchange these things with each other through the instrumentality of this money—and then we should be compelled to stop, for the money would be swallowed up, and all the wealth remaining would have no representative, and no medium through which it might be further divided or exchanged.

Such, then, being the true nature of money, it is apparent that any material agreed upon by the community at large—whether gold, silver, iron, pottery, or paper—would answer every purpose for which money is required. It is not necessary that there should be gold, and that the gold should be a foundation for the paper. All that is requisite for the issuing of paper-money, or any other medium of exchange, is that there should be actual produce of some kind for it to rest upon. There are in the United Kingdom upwards of three millions of buildings, we are possessed of above one hundred and fifty thousand

vessels of various descriptions, and we have likewise an
immense quantity of implements and machinery of different kinds. All these things are real capital—something
to assist in further production. The whole of this wealth
has been calculated to be worth above five thousand millions of pounds sterling. But, under the present system,
this enormous mass of capital cannot be said to have any
representative whatever ; for there is not in the nation a
sum of money equivalent even to one hundred millions
sterling; and yet the whole of this capital, if necessary,
might be represented just as easily as a part.

The comparatively small amount of money now in circulation, with its constant fluctuation, exposes all men to
many injustices, and gives rise to much of the inequality
of condition observed around us. Although it has long
been known that the more money there is in circulation,
the better it is for trade—and that a scarcity of money invariably makes business dull—the economists have never
yet devised any effectual plan for creating a sufficiency of
money. Cost of production, the true standard of exchangeable value, is often, under the present system, completely
lost sight of ; and the value of things is regulated by the
the greater or less quantity of money there is in circulation. For example, a house which at one time is worth
one thousand pounds, is, at another time, worth only nine
hundred—and this, too, when houses are just as necessary
and as truly valuable at the one time as at the other. Thus,
if half of the people in the United Kingdom wished to dis-
pose of their houses and lands at the present moment, for the
purpose of emigrating, they would not be able to sell them.
There is not enough of money in the whole world to purchase them ; and, upon the present principles and system
of trading, and the present action of demand and supply,
the sum which would purchase one house at the beginning
of such a sale, would obtain fifty at the conclusion !

A national medium of exchange, or money, in a social
system where money is requsite, should be in sufficient
quantity to represent the whole of the national fixed capital—the buildings and machinery of every kind—which
can be made available in further production. The real or
inherent value of the circulating medium itself is a matter
of no moment. The only requisite qualities in money are,
that it should be difficult of imitation, portable, capable of

representing larger or smaller values, and durable, or easily replaced; and there is no known substance which possesses ss great a proportion of these qualities as paper.

The durability which is so requsite to a medium in constant circulation—such as the present silver and copper coinage—might be secured by the introduction of a currency of pottery. In the present state of science, a beautiful and efficient medium of this character might easily be created; and while it would possess every requisite of gold, silver, and copper, it might be produced at infinitely less cost, in unlimited quantities, and would be subject to none of the fluctuations which now continually take place in consequence of the transmission of the metals from one country to another. Gold and silver are even now almost unnecessary for transacting the exchanges between Great Britain and other nations; and, under the system of community, they might be totally dispensed with. These metals now flow from country to country more in the shape of commodities than in payment for debts which have been contracted; and this fluctuation, together with their cost of production, and the expenses, attendant on their constant coinage and re-coinage, render them totally unfit for the composition of a circulating medium.

Nations have never yet acted upon any truly systematic plan with respect to their medium of exchange. People seldom think of inquiring how it comes to pass that a small bank-note will buy a suit of clothes, when a newspaper, fifty times as large, will not purchase a loaf of bread. This circumstance does not arise from the preponderating inherent value of the bank-note—for it is not, of itself, worth so much as the newspaper—but it owes its origin simply to the conventional usages of society. The note has been created as a substitute for gold; and common consent has stamped it with a fictitious, a merely representative value, altogether distinct from and independent of its own intrinsic value; and were the positions of the bank-note and the newspaper reversed, the latter would perform all the services now rendered by the former. It is to a like conventional usage, more than to any specific properties of its own, that gold is indebted for its long-maintained supremacy and its universal estimation. When coined, however, it can be regarded only as a representative of real capital; and as the gold thus represents the capital, and the bank-

note represents the gold, there is no earthly reason why
the bank-note should not at once represent the capital,
without the intervention of the gold.

The greater part of the commercial transactions of the
United Kingdom have for many years been carried on by
means of a paper medium—by bank-notes, bills, &c., which
are regarded as representative of gold or capital. But
if all the money now in the country—the gold, silver, and
bills of every kind—were by any means to be suddenly destroyed, the nation would be very little less rich than it is at
present, although it would lose nominal wealth, or money,
of the value of many hundred thousands of pounds sterling. The loss would soon be replaced by the manufacture
of bank-notes and bills of various amounts; and in a short
time business would go on as usual, and the exchange of
commodities would be effected by paper money alone, instead of by a mixed medium of paper and gold. Were
the real capital, however—the buildings and implements
—to disappear or be destroyed, we should be in a state of
greater impoverishment than any beggars now to be found,
even if every man in the country had ten thousand
sovereigns in his pocket. We should be, in the common
acceptation of the term, the richest people in the world,
but, in reality, we should be more poverty-stricken and
miserable than the poorest nation of savages existing.
There would be but one wide picture of want and desolation to be seen among us.

Here it may be seen how utterly valueless are gold and
silver coin and bank-notes, when separated from those
things which only and truly are real wealth. It is this
wealth which gives value to the coin and notes, and not
the money which confers value on the produce created by
labour. It will not for a moment be denied, that if every
working man in the United Kingdom had one hundred
sovereigns put into his pocket, it would make a wonder-
ful difference in the general appearance of society, in
respect to the attainment of work and food. Every man
in need would at once provide himself with necessaries,
and the present gloom would give place to hilarity and
cheerfulness. And yet such an influx of gold would not,
at the moment, make the real wealth of the country greater
by the value of one loaf of bread. But it would give a
vast stimulus to trade, *for it would set thousands to work to*

*replace the commodities of every kind which their sover-
eigns would enable them to purchase and consume.* Parties, also, might combine together and form joint-stock
companies, and set themselves to work at once; and thus
production would receive an impetus such as it has never
yet known. Precisely the same effects would be produced,
if, instead of gold, every man had a like amount of Bank
of England notes. Were there, however, no buildings, or
machinery, or real capital of any kind in the country, by
means of which men might be set to work, any such issue
or possession either of gold or bank-notes would effect no
good whatever. As we are at present situated, such an
increase of money would simply be an increased repre-
sentation of *wealth already in existence,* and it would enable those who now have nothing, to obtain, by exchange,
a portion from those who have a superfluity. But in case
of the non-existence of real capital, the proper foundation
for money, the gold and bank-notes would alike be utterly
worthless, for they would only be, as it were, representatives of *wealth to be created.*

Thus, then, in regard to those social evils dependent on
the existing scarcity of money—it cannot be denied or disproved that there is a universal desire for the comforts
and conveniences of life—that all these things must be
produced by labour—that there is a sufficiency of raw
material to absorb the labour of all—that there is likewise a sufficiency of food for the support of all while they
are engaged in the production of other food, and of all the
other things desired—that labour can be set to work only by
the assistance of capital—that capital may be effectually represented and brought into operation by a paper medium,
—and therefore there is abundant demonstration, that an
indefinite increase of the circulating medium, under particular circumstances, would instantly set labour in motion,
and thus incalculably increase the production of wealth,
and universally diffuse the advantages of such production.
Thousands are now idle and poor because no person can set
them to work—they cannot be set to work simply because
themselves and others are destitute of the requisite money.
There is and there can be no other cause, so long as there
is plenty of labour, an abundance of the raw material, a
sufficiency of machines and implements, and a universal
desire for the necessaries and luxuries of life.

All these considerations respecting the nature and uses of money open a vast field of action for the productive classes, and point out a path by which all their present miseries may be escaped from, and themselves delivered from the soul-blighting dominion of the capitalist. They will find the knowledge of this simple subject to be one of the strongest levers which can ever be made use of by them for the subversion of the present system.

Scarcely a year passes without bringing forth a noise from the camp of the enemies of Labour, respecting the circulating medium, or the " currency." This squabbling and uproar arise while it is being determined between the two parties, whether the landholder capitalist or the commercial capitalist shall have the greatest portion of the national spoil. The working classes are supposed to have nothing to do with the matter, their interests are in no way consulted, nor can they gain anything by the success of the one or the other division of the capitalists; but were the present monetary system clearly seen into by the productive classes, they would take care to have a voice in the decision of the question. Devise what he may, it is impossible for the ingenuity of man to create any instrument which will enable him to exercise such power over his fellow-man as he now obtains by means of the system of banking, or the creation and issue of money. This constitutes the great armoury from whence the capitalists derive all their weapons to fight with and conquer the working class; and so long as they have this mighty engine of good or evil at their disposal—so long as the power of making and issuing money is usurped by particular classes, independent of other classes—the moneyed class can bid defiance to political associations, and trades' unions, and all similar institutions having for their object the amelioration of the condition of the working class, and the effecting of their deliverance from the chains of capital.

That this part of the subject may be more clearly seen into, we have only to examine what the economists themselves say with respect to money:—" The time lost and the trouble incurred in the way of barter, is avoided by the adoption of a medium of exchange—that is, a commodity generally agreed upon, which, in order to effect an exchange between two other commodities, is first *received* in exchange for the one, and then given in exchange for the other." Such is the account given by the economists of the nature and intention of money. In this brief history, however, the first steps of the transactions are kept out of sight, and the last part only of the movement is brought into view. It is not said who originally produces this "commodity generally agreed upon"—this money—and gives it in exchange for the *first* commodity; nor is it told who creates this first commodity for which the money is given. Three parties only are apparently engaged in the transaction—the first having in his possession the "commodity generally agreed upon," and the second and third holding the commodities which they wish to exchange. Herein lies the knavery and mystery of banking and money-making.

The true and only meaning of the quotation just given, is, that certain parties produce or make a medium of exchange, or money, for which *they receive commodities.* Now, if the medium of exchange thus given for the *commodity* be of equal value with the commodity, the exchange is a just one; but if it be of inferior value, or of no value whatever, the transaction is a robbery on the part of those by whom the medium is made. For two things to be of equal value in exchange, their cost of production must be equal. The common circulating medium is composed of paper and gold—the first all but worthless, and the last deriving its chief value from the quantity of labour required for its production. We have already seen that the capitalists do not labour, and that, consequently, they can produce nothing; but as the gold can be originally obtained only by means of labour, the capitalists can have nothing to do with its production. The gold, however, has come into possession of the capitalists; and therefore they must, in their exchanges, either have defrauded the parties who at first produced the gold, or else they have defrauded the parties from whom they obtained the commodities given by them in exchange for the gold. The barbarities and injustice connected with the production of gold are notorious enough; but it is the second transaction which more nearly concerns the productive classes of the United Kingdom. The present circulating medium, then, as the economists confess, is made by a class of capitalists called bankers—some of them acting independently, and others in connection with the established government—and for this medium of exchange, or money, it is acknowledged that the bankers receive commodities of certain parties. These *second* parties, in turn, exchange the money for other commodities from some *third* party ; and upon the same principle, of giving value for value, the exchange goes on among all succeeding parties. Thus *real value* is rendered in exchange for real value in every case except the *first transaction*—that between the banker and the person who receives his medium—and in this first negociation, according to the showing even of the economists, there is a vile and cunning robbery committed upon the productive classes ; for it plainly appears that the *makers* of the medium—the bankers, capitalists and other feeders upon the industry of the working class—render *no real equivalent* for the commodities which they receive in exchange for their medium. The great majority of the *borrowers* of the medium belong to the same unproductive class as the makers of it ; and the wealth which they give as interest, or as an equivalent for the use of the money borrowed, is what they have previously obtained from the working class, by means of unequal exchanges! Thus the productive classes give to the banking and the trading capitalists their labour—their very sweat and blood—and the latter give to them, in exchange—what? They give them a shadow—a rag—a " bank-note !"

The creation of a circulating medium is, under the present system, just as much a trade as the making of shoes or hats. A person, or a number of persons, with or without property, can at any time establish a bank and issue money by conforming to certain regulations. For instance, a thousand persons join together to establish a joint-stock bank, which is to be possessed of a capital of the value of £1,000,000, in one thousand shares at £1,000 each. If these parties possess, or be supposed to possess, real property of the value of their respective shares, they can forthwith make and issue bank-notes of the nominal value of one million of pounds sterling, although there may not be amongst the whole of them even the one-thousandth part of this sum in gold. The bank-notes, however, imply that they may at any time be exchanged for gold at the bank from whence they have been issued ; and they are taken by the public on this security, although it is almost universally known that there is never in the coffers of a bank one-half the quantity of gold which would be required to cash the notes issued. It is supposed that there is in the hands of the proprietors real capital or created wealth which will at any time sell for the whole sum issued by the bank ; and hundreds of persons daily deposit their hard-earned savings in these banks on a security which, in innumerable instances, has been found utterly worthless, and the failure of which has brought ruin and beggary on thousands.

When the bank commences operations, a farmer or tradesman, whether with or without property, can, if of good credit, get an advance of bank-notes from the bankers. For the use of these notes he gives to the bankers a sum varying from five to ten pounds per hundred on the money borrowed, according to the time the money is kept by him. Thus, if a man borrow the sum of £100 for a twelvemonth, at ten per cent. interest, he pays to the banker, at the expiration of this time, the sum of £110—thereby giving £10 more than he received. According to the number of borrowers the bankers have in this manner, they become more or less rich ; and, if a capital of £1,000,000 be fully employed, at five per cent. per annum, it will yearly bring in the sum of £5,000—and this, too, without labour of any kind on the part of the mere proprietors, and with very little deterioration of the original stock ! The persons who borrow the notes—whether tradesmen or speculators—set other men to work by means of this money, or buy commodities with it at a low price and sell them at a high price ; and thus, no matter whether it be by giving a low price for labour and selling its produce at a high price, or by purchasing commodities cheap and selling them dear, the tradesmen and speculators are not only enabled to give the banker £110 for the £100 borrowed from him, but they are also enabled to live in affluence with little or no labour of their own.

Here it is seen, at a glance, how it happens that such enormous fortunes—such millions and half-millions sterling—are acquired by men who originally possessed not one penny, and who have never produced real wealth of the value of one farthing. Such is the system of banking —such is the manner in which this system benefits *those*

who make the medium and those who borrow it; and this
mode of creating and using money is alone sufficient, in
defiance alike of trades' combinations and political changes,
to keep the working class the slaves of the capitalists until
doomsday.

This great wrong is part and parcel of that social system, through the instrumentality of which the productive
classes are annually plundered of wealth to the amount of
three hundred millions sterling. It is one of the manifestations of the principle of unequal exchanges—it is one
of the masterly inventions framed to cloak and conceal the
treacheries of Capital towards Labour. So long as money
is thus made and issued and borrowed by individuals and
classes, it will tend to individual and class benefit—it will
separate society into rich idlers and poor workers—it will
bind Labour in fetters as durable as the system itself.

Daily experience, apart from any reasoning on the subject, teaches all men that the power of the capitalist does
not arise from any mental or physical superiority possessed
by his class over other classes; for, as a body, this class is
notoriously deficient in the higher attributes of existence.
They are powerful simply because they are possessed of
money—the representative of the things which the working classes have produced—for this money always enables
the capitalists to command everything which is represented by it. Thousands of instances are on record of
men of very meagre capacity commencing and carrying on
immense businesses, and growing enormously rich, simply
by means of borrowing the representative—*and borrowing
it, too, from parties afterwards proved to have been as destitute of real wealth as the borrowers themselves were!*
But the whole of the wealth acquired in this manner—
the per centage of the banker as well as the profit of the
tradesman and speculator—comes entirely from the productive classes, and is obtained from them by means of
unequal exchanges. The present system throughout affords
the capitalist every possible facility for preying upon the
producer; for it is a vile compound of conventional usages
which enable him to grind, without ceasing, the face of
the working man.

There can, under the present arrangements of society,
be no alteration in this state of things that will be beneficial to the working class. It matters not to them whe-

ther the money thus made and issued come from a private
or a national bank. In the first case, the class from which
the money comes will ever constitute a wrong. If the
capitalists dug for gold in the bowels of the earth, and
thus exchanged their own labour against the labour of
others, the transaction between them and the working men
would be a foolish one, but there would be no injustice in
it. But the capitalists neither dig nor beg. They issue a
medium, for which they receive commodities, and these
commodities they give in exchange for the gold. Thus
neither the gold nor the commodities cost the capitalist
any labour. It matters not, in regard to its general effects,
whether the medium of a banker be issued and continued
on a real or a nominal capital. The public faith is all that
the banker needs. If isolated private banks give place to
a national bank, the profits of which are devoted to public
purposes, the case will be but little better for the working
class. Their position in society, under the present system,
will ever prevent them from receiving any material benefit
from such an institution. *They* can never be borrowers—
they will never be able to work with such capital on their
own account and for their own benefit—but they will still
be set to work by others, and the profits of their labour
will be appropriated and enjoyed by others.

Not content with thus plundering the producers on all
sides, the capitalists, with a refinement in cunning until
recently unknown, have actually succeeded in making the
working class the willing instruments of their own degradation. As bank-notes have always professed to be
exchangeable for gold, and are ever going back to the
bank for such purpose, it is apparent that every bank must
have a supply of gold adequate to meet these minor
demands. The greater the number of banks, therefore,
or the larger the amount of their paper issues, the more
necessary is it that a considerable amount of gold should
be at hand to meet emergencies. The great body of the
producers work for weekly wages, which are paid in gold
or silver; and as many thousands of them do not consume
all that they thus receive, there will be a residue left on
hand to be used as occasions require. The incessant hoarding even of 1s. a week, by a few hundreds of thousands of
persons, will in the course of a year amount to a considerable sum; and as this is drawn from the circulation, the

stocks of metal in the banks decrease, and the bankers find it difficult to meet the demand for coin. There is in the United Kingdom a government bank, called the Bank of England, which may be regarded as the great fountain from whence the other banks derive their golden stores. This bank has ever suffered, in common with others, from any deficiency in its amount of gold; and to remedy this inconvenience, and at the same time increase the profits of the bank, and give the government a better hold upon a discontented population, some cunning brain devised a " Savings' Bank"—a triple engine of power in the hands of Capital and Despotism. Through the instrumentality of this invention, the coffers of the bankers receive back the specie almost as fast as it is taken from them—the government bankers extract a large revenue from the pro-ductive classes by *allowing the capitalists to make use of their money*—and the government itself holds, as it were, so many golden chains to bind men to it and to the exist-ing order of things.

The government now owes to the productive classes, for money thus deposited in Savings' Banks, a sum of above £14,000,000 sterling—a sum which, if applied to the sub-version instead of the continuance of the present social system, would make a breach that no power could repair. The greater part of this sum has been deposited in gold and silver, and specie is therefore expected back again when wanted; but there is not in possession of all the banks in the country specie equivalent to meet the demands on the Savings' Bank. Thus this money may be regarded as all but lost to those who deposited it in the hands of the government; and although a timely application would secure a part, some persons must eventually go without. The present has been called an age of revolutions, and the overthrow of dynasties and the partition of kingdoms are yearly heard of; and should any event take place in the United Kingdom calculated to shake public confidence or cause internal commotions, and thus send the productive classes in droves for their money, an immediate stoppage would be put to all refunding—and distress and starvation would be left to work out their own cure, unalleviated by the assistance of former savings. That such a restriction of the issues of coin would *probably* be the case, may be inferred from experience, the same stoppage of the supplies

having been resorted to on former and similar occasions—
that such would *most certainly* be the case, is self-evident
from the fact, that the amount of specie wanted is neither
in the hands of nor in any way procurable by the government; and if *paper* be given by them, it has been already
shewn that *nothing* will be given.

Thus, for the trifling bait—the so-called "interest"—of
6d. per annum for the use of £1, the productive classes are
ignorantly led not only to provide the capitalists with weapons to conquer them, but likewise to endanger or lose
entirely the miserable pittance which years of denial have
enabled them to accumulate. But were these united savings
applied to the purchase of real capital, and the employment
of the working classes *by and for themselves,* on the system of community of possessions and equality of rights,
there would be introduced into the present system a power
sufficient speedily to overthrow it, and to hurl down and
destroy the dominion of Labour's enemies.

Under the present arrangements of society, money is, as
it were, a chain of communication between the positive and
the negative—between those who produce everything and
those who produce nothing—between the working man and
the capitalist. Through its instrumentality, all that is
generated by the power of labour is perpetually carried
off, and absorbed by capital. There is in things a principle
which keeps them in equilibrium with each other; and
when one receives a property of which it was before destitute, it parts with some other property in exchange. This
law holds good even between the capitalist and the producer; and the latter receives, in exchange for what he
gives to the capitalist—not the labour nor the produce of
the labour of the capitalist, but—work! Through the
instrumentality of money, the working class are not only
compelled to perform the labour which the preservation of
existence naturally imposes upon them, but they are likewise saddled with *the labour of other classes.* It matters
not whether the producers now receive gold, or silver, or
other commodities from a non-producing class: it all
amounts to this—that the working class perform *their
own labour, and support themselves, and likewise perform
the labour of the capitalist, and maintain him into the
bargain !* Whatever may be the nominal receipts which
the producers receive from the capitalists, their actual

receipts are—the transfer of that labour which ought to be rendered by the capitalists.

Such, then, is money—such is the mode in which it is created—such are the evils and the wrongs inseparable from its existence, so long as it is created and used by particular classes, to the exclusion of other classes. Such exclusiveness must ever compel the working class to be the slaves and the tools of their fellows ; and the seal of their doom can be broken asunder only by a power which at the same time overthrows the present system.

CHAPTER XI.

AN OUTLINE OF A SOCIAL MOVEMENT.

IF sufficient proof has not been given of the corrupt tendencies and the unimprovable character of the present system, those who wish for more evidence have not far to look for it. Let us go where we will—see and hear what we will—read of the past and the present what we will—all places, actions, and times, have the same tale to tell. History and experience bear evidence, in characters of fire, and blood, and misery, that this social system never has been, is not now, and never can be, anything but a dark and chaotic sea of evil, in which oppression is unpunished, virtue and morality unregarded, merit unrewarded, and the tears of the widow and the orphan unpitied and unheeded. Thus, from its very nature, and the irremediable evils connected with it, there is nothing to induce us to retain the present system, even were its subversion attended by treble the difficulty which stands in the way of its accomplishment.

Changes are ever taking place, more or less important in regard to their effects upon society. Man is a progressing being; and he looks to the past, therefore, not so much to take pattern of that which was good, as to derive warning from that which was evil. In regard to any forward move_ment which may be made, the considerations which have been already entered into respecting what is well and what is ill in the present system, and what is requisite to the establishment and the progression of a better system, will enable us to determine what should be given up and what retained. Keeping all these things in view, we can at once briefly proceed to the consideration of a mode of subvert_ing the present system, independent alike of change of character or the accumulation of capital among those making the attempt—two requisites almost indispensable to the success of any of the plans which have been examined.

Of the six millions of adult men in the United King_dom, it has been calculated that about five millions assist in producing and distributing wealth; and that of this num_ber, four millions belong to the division called the working class. It has been shewn that, by the present arrange_ments of society, this last great division receive scarcely £200,000,000 of the £500,000,000 of wealth annually created, which averages about £11 per head for the men, women, and children comprised in this class; and that for this miserable pittance they toil, on the average, 11 hours a day.

A consideration of the principles of production has shewn us, that three things only are necessary to the crea_tion of any amount of wealth, namely, raw material, labour, and capital; and it has likewise taught us the best means of regulating the various powers at our disposal—by union of forces and division of labour—so as to produce the greatest quantity of wealth with the least expenditure of capital and labour. The best exemplification of the power which man may wield by union of forces and divi_sion of labour, is afforded by the working of a joint-stock company. These companies are usurping, in all directions the places and occupations hitherto confined to individual capitalists and traders; and the systematic and extended manner in which this joint-stock system of trading has been acted upon during late years, has given almost every person some knowledge of the principles and mode of action from which its strength is derived. The gigantic power of such companies is beheld in innumerable roads, railways, and canals, and in the creation and distribution of almost every description of wealth. It is known that the power of these companies arises solely from the skilful application of capital and labour; and it is self-evident that the like application of capital and labour, under similar circumstances, will ever produce similar results.

We have already, as it were, taken stock of the real capital and the employed and unemployed labour in the United Kingdom. We have found the capital to be worth no less than five thousand millions sterling, which, under present arrangements, gives employment only to about four millions of working men and one million of half-employed distributors—thus leaving unused and mis-used the effective strength of one million of men, in connection with uncultivated land, and unemployed machinery and tools, in every factory and workshop, sufficient to fill the hands of all men. Thousands now starve in unproductive inaction because the capitalist cannot employ them—the capitalist cannot give them work because he cannot find a market for his produce—there is no market for the produce because those who want the produce have nothing but their labour to give in exchange for it—and their labour is unemployed because the capitalist does not know how to set them to work—and thus the evils of the present system run round in a circle, one connected with and dependent upon another, and every one individually incurable.

Therefore, in respect to a social change:—it is not disputed that there is in the United Kingdom a sufficiency of the raw material of wealth to employ all the labour which can be brought to bear upon it—it is universally known that there are tens of thousands of half-starved men in unproductive inaction—it has been proved, by flushes of trade at different times, that there are implements and machines to fill the hands of all—the experience of many years has proved that there is generally food enough in the country to support comfortably all the inhabitants from one harvest to another, and that any amount can be had by exchanging our productions for the corn of foreign countries—it has been shewn that a medium of exchange, or money, can be manufactured in such abundance as to set in motion all the unemployed labour and implements in the country—and as there are all these requisites and facilities, why should they not be made a proper use of, and all the advantages obtained which can be made to result from the combined operation of so many powers?

Without, for the present, entering into a consideration of the possibility of effecting this change, let it for a moment be supposed that the whole five millions of the adult producers in the United Kingdom are formed into a number of joint-stock companies, containing from 100 to 1,000 men each, according to locality and other circumstances—that each of these companies is comprised of men of one trade, or confines its attention to the production or distribution of particular commodities—that these companies have in use, by hire or purchase, the land and fixed capital of the country—that they are set in motion and kept moving by a circulating bank-note capital equivalent to £100 for each associated member of the community, which, taking into account the women and children connected with the five millions of producers, will comprise, altogether, about twenty millions of individuals, and a capital of two thousand millions sterling. Supposing the productive classes of the United Kingdom to be thus associated together, for the production and distribution of wealth—that they trade together with a floating capital of £2,000,000,000— that all their affairs are conducted through the instrumentality of general and local boards of trade, comprised of the most able and business-like men that can be found— that the members of all the companies, after the manner of the present system, are paid weekly wages for their labour—what is there now accomplished in respect to production and distribution, either by joint-stock companies or individual capitalists, which could not likewise be accomplished by the productive classes thus associated? The wonders which are wrought everywhere around us, by means of joint-stock companies, shew what even a very limited union of forces is capable of accomplishing; and if individual and unallied companies can effect thus much, what may not be achieved by the united powers of thousands of such companies—all having a common interest, working for a common end, and deriving a common benefit from all that is produced?

A few very simple arrangements would enable a change like this to be effected; and such a change would at once set in motion the whole of the unemployed labour in the empire—it would, without inflicting injury on any trade or any individual, allow of the introduction of an unlimited quantity of machinery—and the power of this gigantic union of labour and machinery would be maintained by a circulating medium of two thousand millions of pounds sterling. The imagination, chained down to the molehill mountains of the present system, cannot at once embrace the vast prospect and the almost omnipotent powers unfolded in a change like this!

A social movement of this character would require no fundamental alteration in disposition, or character, or habits, in the parties acting. There are no new feelings to be acquired, no old associations to be shaken off, more than would be requisite in any simple governmental change, such as men are yearly subjected to. The whole movement would require only co-operation in its simplest form, such as at the present moment exists in every trade and in every workshop, where persons of the widest extremes in respect to character, strength, and opinion, harmoniously co-operate together to effect some definite object in production. The path to action is thus already prepared, and we should only have to go forward, as it were, upon a beaten and a well-known road.

Competition could have no existence in a change like this ; and the economists, considering competition as the mainspring of production, unhesitatingly predict that any social arrangements which take away this stimulus—which remove the fear of future want or the hope of future gain—will be injurious to production, and subversive of the prosperity and harmony of society. Instances are brought forward to shew that, in proportion as men are secured against the future, they relax in their endeavours, and become careless of labour, and of the production of wealth—that men are not so willing to exert themselves in procuring that which will be enjoyed by all, as if the enjoyment were confined exclusively to themselves—that when production is the business of every body it is the business of nobody, and each man endeavours to escape at the expense of his neighbours.

Although the testimony of experience goes to prove the general truth of these objections, when they are applied to the world as it is, it has been shewn that they have no force when opposed to a social system combining a change of character and new social arrangements, or to the joint-stock modification now under consideration. Competition is only a secondary cause of production; for men compete with each other for the possession of certain things, because they desire these things, and because, under the present system, *they can obtain them only by competition.* It is the natural desire for things, and not the competition, which originally incites men to action; and so long as this desire exists, production will go forward efficiently, unallied with and independent of competition. If there were plenty of work for all men, there would now be no competition for it; nor would there be any competition for the possession of particular commodities, if there were a sufficiency of every thing produced to supply the wants of all; and yet men would work together, and produce commodities in greater abundance, and enjoy themselves in a far greater degree, in such a state of things, than if one-half of them were idle, and the other half, by competition, were reduced to the necessity of labouring for what may be called a nominal existence. Competition, likewise, can be dispensed with as a stimulant to enterprise and invention; for it is notorious that the majority of inventors and intellectual labourers, instead of expecting or receiving any reward, now live and die in a state of poverty and misery exceeding even that of the most mindless being who makes use of their discoveries. If it be contended that men will not do their duty to their fellows without being spurred on by a stimulus more or less connected with their animal wants—that if the men of all trades and professions receive one uniform rate of wages, a carelessness will be engendered as to whether much or little is produced—that if all be insured a future provision, they will become indifferent to present exertion—if these and similar arguments be brought forward against the contemplated change, they will be of no more weight than if applied to individuals under the present system. Under the joint-stock movement, there will be all the incentives to action which exist at present—there will be a Public Opinion to give its award to particular actions—and the provision for the future will, as is now the case, depend upon the labour of the past. In almost all trades, the workmen now receive a stated weekly sum, although the powers of production of various individuals differ considerably; and yet such uniformity in the rate of payment does not encourage idleness.

The opinion entertained of a man by his fellow-workmen is generally sufficient to excite him to honest exertions; and the advantages held out by the joint-stock system—in which every person would ultimately receive *the whole* fruits of his labour—are so superior to any now enjoyed, that they could not fail to create one universal spirit of enterprise and activity.

It can be easily determined in what manner such a system would work in regard to individuals and to society at large. We have already supposed that an indefinite number of joint-stock companies are formed—that their transactions are governed by general and local boards of trade, which would regulate production and distribution in gross —that their minor details are superintended by managers and overlookers, as at present—that the members of these companies work the same number of hours and receive one uniform rate of wages. Under the present system, the hours of labour vary from eighty to forty, and the wages from fifty to ten shillings per week; but in scarcely any instance have the wages any dependence on the hours of labour, for it generally happens that those receive the least wages who work the greatest number of hours. Under the joint-stock system, however, so great would be the amount of labour and machinery of every kind set in motion, that, in a short time, sufficient wealth would be produced for the enjoyment of all persons by an expenditure of not more than five hours' labour a day. But even at its first institution, it would require no more than from eight to ten hours' labour per day from each associated producer; and this moderate exertion would yield him an equivalent equal to two shillings an hour. Cost of production would in every instance determine value; and equal values would always exchange for equal values. If one person worked a whole week, and another worked only half a week, the first would receive double the remuneration of the last; but this extra pay of the one would not be at the expense of the other, nor would the loss incurred by the last man fall in any way upon the first. Each person would exchange the wages he individually received, for commodities of the same value as his respective wages; and in no case could the gain of one man or one trade be a loss to another man or another trade. The labour of every individual would alone determine his gains and his losses.

The arrangements respecting the production of food

could be adjusted on the same principle of equality as would prevail in manufactures of various kinds. As the land, like the houses and machinery, would be held as common property, the value of all its products would be estimated on an equitable principle, such as should afford equal advantages to every member of society. Those employed in agriculture would be remunerated according to their labour, and not by amount of crop ; and society at large would receive the benefit, or bear the loss, of productive or unproductive seasons.

Under this joint-stock modification of society, as under a more perfect system, ample provision could be made for the young, the aged, and the infirm, without subjecting parents or relatives to the least trouble or anxiety. With regard to employment, every company would be open to the admission of persons whose labour had been superseded by machinery ; and who, by being immediately provided with a suitable occupation, would neither suffer loss themselves, nor inflict an injury upon society. There is so much of all kinds of work to be done, that there never can be too much labour set at liberty, or superseded by machinery. But if any man, or any body of men, be made to suffer from an improvement which confers a benefit upon society at large, an act of gross injustice is committed ; for as every individual ought to confer as much benefit as possible upon society, so, likewise, is society equally bound to contribute to the welfare of all its members. But society can do this only by instituting such social arangements as, while they enforce the principle and practice of universal labour, *take care that employment shall always be procurable.* It is easy enough for the overgorged capitalist to say to the working man whose labour, under the present system, has been superseded by machinery—" Turn to some other employment !" The world now offers the workman no such employment, and he is therefore compelled to combat against his steam and iron adversaries until he is worked to death, or perishes from disease and starvation.

At the present time, it would be useless to enter into minute details of what could and what should be done under a new social system such as that under consideration. We have experience to guide us in almost every thing ; for the present movement is not an introduction of new principles and modes of action, but simply the application of existing principles and modes to a new object—the universal and equal benefit of society at large, instead of the aggrandisement of particular individuals and classes. There is always, if it be rightly managed, a fund of common sense in the world sufficient for all emergencies. Almost every man is aware of the order and precision with which the transactions of companies and individuals are at present carried on, however extensive or complicated they may be. By means of general and local boards of trade, and the directors attached to each individual company, the quantities of the various commodities required for consumption—the relative value of each in regard to each other—the number of hands required in various trades and descriptions of labour—and all other matters connected with production and distribution, could in a short time be as easily determined for a nation as for an individual company under the present arrangements. Statistics of every kind would acquire a degree of correctness and perfection such as they can never attain to under the existing system. The simple principles of equality are of such a nature that they can be acted upon in all transactions and all emergencies; for, like the compass of the mariner, they can guide alike in the darkness as in the sunshine—in the storm as in the calm.

The social change under consideration, great and beneficial as would be its own immediate effects, would be an easy preparatory step to the more perfect change already considered. There is nothing in the movement which can arouse the fears of the most faint-hearted. It is not to be expected that society can become perfect at once—that the vicious propensities and wrong notions which have grown with our growth and strengthened with our strength, can be eradicated or changed in a moment. But as comparative wealth and increased leisure shall take the place of hopeless poverty and inordinate toil—when better arrangements than those which now exist shall diffuse education universally—when the present narrow views and warped sympathies of classes shall be expanded and adjusted, and men made to regard all their fellows as members of one great family, having a common interest and progressing towards a common end—then will society gradually and imperceptibly glide into the state desired, and establish those institutions and usages which are so essential to the highest scale of civilization.

Every whole is but an aggregate of parts, and a nation will ever be broken up into communities or divisions of some kind. As individuals compose families, and families towns, under the existing system, so likewise would they after the joint-stock change had been effected. The present distribution of people in towns and villages, bad as it is, would not be directly interfered with ; nor would there be any immediate destruction and re-erection of the buildings now in existence, unhealthy and uncomfortable as they are. We have all, more or less, imbibed feelings of attachment to our present habits, pursuits, and modes of action. We are thus morally incapacitated from acting upon a more perfect division of society into communities comprised of many families, in which there is but one feeling and one manner of living. It is not pretended that society, in these days, has knowledge enough, or morality enough, or honesty enough, for such a system. The trammelled minds of men cannot yet grasp the great and glorious destiny which is conceived for them in the womb of the future. But if perfection cannot be attained at once, there is nothing to deter men from planting the seed of future good.

Although society will ever be broken up into parts, it does not necessarily follow that those parts shall always maintain the same jarring and hostile relation to each other as they now do, and always will do, when classified as rich and poor. Man is not naturally the enemy of man ; nor would he ever be so, if the interest of one were not opposed to the interest of another. This opposition of interests does not exist in joint-stock companies. If one shareholder gain or lose anything by a company, all the other members do so likewise ; and this universality and equality of interest at present exists under no other circumstances. Thus, either under the joint-stock division of society, or in any other modification of the principle of community, where labour is universal and remuneration in proportion to the labour, the interest of any one man will be equally the interest of all ; and this reciprocity and equality of interests would extend from one company to all.

Thus, taking society as we find it—with all its irrational habits and prejudices, its ill-arranged and incommodious habitations and modes of production, its depraved tastes and ignorant appliances of the means of enjoyment —no arrangements can bring into operation powers so extensive in their application and gigantic in their results, as those existing in connection with a joint-stock modification of the principle of community of possessions. Such a system would be simple and effectual in regard to the creation and distribution of wealth—it would, as far as possible, insure equality of exchanges, and give to every man that true independence which, under the present system, must ever be unknown to the workman—it would instantly alleviate the poverty, and crime, and vicious habits, produced by too little and too much work—it would allow of a comfortable provision for the young, the old, and the infirm, without discomfort to themselves or loss to the community. Under such social arrangements, one class would not, as at present, be dependent upon another for employment ; nor could the gains of one man be an accumulation of the losses of another.

The objections which have been urged by the economists against the more perfect system of community of possessions, do not apply to this joint-stock modification of the principle. The present could not be called the trying of a mere experiment—the feeling of our way in the dark—the precursor of universal apathy, and poverty, and immorality. Throughout this change, society would act upon well-known principles—principles which the experience of every day proves to be the more efficacious and powerful in proportion as they are the more extensively acted upon. It would be simply an extension of the union of a few individuals, to effect a definite object, into the alliance of the people of a nation, to effect the same object ; and as a joint-stock company is stronger than an individual, so will a nation of such companies be superior to any isolated combination.

The production and distribution of an unlimited quantity of wealth, although the first, is not the only requisite to the welfare of society. The next class of arrangements of importance are those relating to education as a whole—to the moral and physical culture of man—to the teaching him his rights and his duties—to the entire formation of his character. Under the joint-stock modification of society, this great object could be speedily and effectually attained. The time and the means which are now so ill-applied to this purpose, could be at once turned into a proper channel, and be indefinitely increased—the demoralizing circumstances which now more or less surround and influence every human being from birth to death, would shortly cease to have existence—and, by a few simple arrangements, every child might receive the best training without either trouble or anxiety on the part of its parents, or loss to the community at large.

In connection with this joint-stock system, as well as in the more perfect form of community, arrangements might be made for the support of women and children, without the former being dependent on their husbands, or the latter on their parents, for the means of subsistence. When rationally viewed, the maintenance and education of children by their parents is a glaring defect in every social system in which the practice prevails. It may be affirmed, truly enough, that all parents have a natural desire to provide for their offspring—that the same stimulus to parental exertion exists even among animals—and it may be from hence inferred, that, by establishing institutions which throw this burthen upon society at large, we act contrary to, and endeavour to subvert, the natural desires of the human breast. Such an objection as this arises from a contracted view of the subject. The inherent feelings of parents can never be annihilated, either in human beings or in brutes ; but it does not follow, because mankind happen to have these feelings in common with brutes, that they should act in the same manner, and individually provide for the childhood of their little ones. We are placed in a very different position, in respect to means, to that of any class of beings around us ; and we are possessed of much higher faculties than those enjoyed by any of the modifications of intelligence with which we are acquainted. We take pattern by them in nothing ; and although man and brute are alike possessed of similar natural feelings in regard to their offspring, yet, while the brute is guided in the preservation of its young by instinct only, man has reason as well as instinct to direct him. Thus, while instinct ever compels human beings to provide for their children, reason only can direct them how to do this in the most effectual manner.

Experience, fraught with innumerable troubles and sorrows, shews every parent—and especially every parent in the productive class—how lamentably imperfect are the present arrangements of society for the protection and welfare of children. The greater part of the sum total of human discomfort is now comprised of parental anxiety for the preservation and happiness of offspring. In consideration of his children, how long and patiently does the workman toil—how many of the insolences of upstart authority does he silently receive—how enduringly does he bear the galling of every chain which the present accursed system fastens upon him! Although solicitude will ever exist, yet fear and doubt, respecting the welfare of their children are no ingredients in parental happiness. By the present irrational arrangements of society, mankind are degraded to the level of brutes,—over which they suffer their boasted reason to give them no pre-eminence, in respect to the preservation of their offspring. Society, when viewed as a whole—in its composition, its constitution, and its intention—ought to know, as society, of no such limited distinctions as those of parents and children. Every child ought to be regarded and protected as the child of society; and society, in its turn, ought to be as a helping child to every aged parent. Every individual, besides his natural relationship to other individuals, has a relationship likewise to society at large; and society, by instituting arrangements for the punishment or protection of its members, tacitly acknowledges this relationship even under the present system. But under a rational organization of society, the immediate dependence of children upon their parents would be, as it ought to be, entirely done away with; and society, taking upon itself the physical, moral, and intellectual culture of all its foster-children, would leave to their parents, as individuals, no offices to perform but the caressings of parental love.

There can be neither wrong nor loss inflicted upon society by thus maintaining its children. The considerations which have been already entered into respecting the nature and origin of wealth, and the experience which man has of his powers of production, go to shew, that, while there is a sufficiency of raw material there never can be too much labour. Every child contains in embryo more or less of labour, mental and corporeal; and consequently, under arrangements which enforce universal labour, and at the same time keep in view the accumulation of sufficient capital to set this labour in motion as it arrives, every child, instead of being a loss, will be a profit to society. It is society, and not the individual parents, which receives the benefits arising from the male and female children born into the world; and upon society, therefore, have they a just claim for an outfit. There would exist under the social system of community, none of the incentives to celibacy which now influence so many thousands. The facility for marriage would be co-extensive with the desire for it. All parents would contribute to the support of all children, in an indirect manner, through proper social regulations; and thus children would not be, as at present, unjustly visited and punished by the sins of their parents.

Bad as are the social arrangements which leave children immediately dependent upon their parents for education and subsistence, a still worse feature in the present system, and one productive of the greater part of the demoralization and vice which surround us, is that custom of society which leaves woman dependent upon individual man for subsistence. Woman should be altogether as independent of man, in respect to her occupation and her maintenance, as man is independent of her or of his fellow-man. Woman is not naturally, and never can be legally, the slave or the property of man; but, in regard to every right appertaining to human existence, she stands with man on a footing of the most perfect equality. Under the present system, woman is dependent upon and is regarded as inferior to man—she is by turns his slave and his plaything—she has no equal social rights, and no political existence. Spoiled by a pernicious and deficient education, half-despised for the apparent want of those mental powers which are not permitted to be called forth and exercised, and degraded by her dependent position,—woman is now fixed in a labyrinth of tyranny and injustice from which she cannot be rescued by any means which do not afford her entire independence of the control of her self-styled superior, in the same degree as he is independent of her. When released from such dominion—when relieved from the fear of future want, and made a co-equal with man— when fostered and protected by social institutions calculated to make her physically, morally, and mentally, what she should be—then will she stand in her true position—

then will the unknown and now unappreciable treasures of her heart and mind be poured out, and she will be to man " a help-mate meet for him."

This joint-stock modification of society would in a short time prepare the way for the introduction of social arrangements calculated to effect all these objects, and every other which philanthropy can desire and intellect discover for the happiness of society. There is ample scope afforded, for philosophical inquiry, and invention, and experiment, by the establishment of national institutions provided with every requisite that unfettered ingenuity and labour can bring into existence. Old age and impotency could be provided for in a manner such as worn-out Labour well deserves for the honest exertions of its better days—and this, too, as a matter of right, and apart from all the feelings now existing in connexion with charity and alms-houses. All losses to individuals and companies, by fire, shipwreck, and other disasters, could be made, as in justice they ought, to fall upon society at large. There would be one great gainer and one great loser—the nation—for society would form, as it were, one vast insurance company, in which the profits only would be known, and the losses be unfelt and unseen.

Upon the establishment of such a system, every social, political, and ecclesiastical grievance under which men now suffer, and with which they have ineffectually combated for centuries, would be almost instantly annihilated. Intolerance would give place to liberality ; and a just, natural, and rational equality of rights and possessions would succeed the present system of exaltations and abasements—of tyranny and slavery—wherein the hand of every man is raised against his fellow, and a wide-spread conventional hypocrisy of love exists in the place of that sympathy and kindness which nature prompts us to entertain towards each other. Under this joint-stock system, the same as under that now existing, every individual would be at liberty to accumulate as much as he pleased, and to enjoy such accumulations when and where he might think proper. The savings of every man would be his own, and would in no way affect the savings of his fellow ; for equal exchanges, and individual independence of individual, render wealth an almost powerless instrument of mischief. By the imposition of a direct tax on individuals or on articles of consumption, together with the rents of buildings, &c., ample funds could be secured to meet all the expenses connected with the proper government of society, the education of all its children, the maintenance of the infirm, the prosecution of scientific research, the progressive demolition and re-erection of the habitations now in existence, the formation of roads, and the establishment of every institution required to meet the wants and the exigencies of society.

Thus, with a social change like this, although the face of society would retain for a time, its present appearance, its whole inner constitution would be daily undergoing a purification, a reviviscency, which would shortly extend to its outward aspect. The abominable wickedness and vice of every kind—the unmitigated moral putrescency—which now exists in the very heart's core of society, and stinks in the nostrils of Truth and Justice, would speedily give place to a purity and vitality such as society has never yet enjoyed ; and the swelling torrent of human happiness, flowing from the rock of right, would bound from heart to heart, until all had drunk of its waters and felt their soul-cheering influence.

To those, then, who deem that a social change is necessary, and to those who decry all such changes as the hallucinations of misguided visionaries or the artful impositions of designing miscreants, the outline of a social movement is before them for consideration. Founded as it is upon established principles of production, and acting throughout upon a well-known and well-tried plan of operations, there can be little doubt that it would tend to the speedy progression of the human race towards that ultimate degree of happiness and perfectibility by which all finite things are bounded. Such a change would give increased wealth and increased leisure to society at large, and thereby remove the poverty and ignorance which now exist—it would be destructive of the present class and caste division of society, as well as of the social and governmental tyranny engendered by this division—and, by allowing of the introduction of circumstantial regulations favourable to the object in view, would enable all persons to acquire a degree of physical, moral, and intellectual excellence to which, under the present system, they can never attain.

A change like this, as well as the more perfect change already considered, presupposes that all the real capital of the country — the land, buildings, machinery, vessels, and every other description of reproducible wealth, except the personal property of individuals — is possessed and controlled by society at large ; that the occupations and authority of the present capitalists and employers, in their individualized capacity, are superseded ; that society is, as it were, one great joint-stock company, composed of an indefinite number of smaller companies, all labouring, producing, and exchanging with each other on terms of the most perfect equality. The idea of such a thing is easily conceived ; and to act upon the conception will be as easy a matter as to conceive it.

Hitherto, we have regarded this social movement only as an established change, without taking into consideration the means whereby such a change is to be accomplished, and the real capital of the country obtained possession of by the productive classes. It has been shewn that, under the present system, wealth is acquired by individuals in two ways—by labour, and by trading—the first being dependent on its own exertions, and the latter being derived, by unequal exchanges, from the exertions of others. Gold and silver coin and bank-notes are the exponents of wealth ; and when a man has obtained possession of these—no matter by what means—he can find multitudes of persons willing to give him lands, houses, or anything else, in exchange for his coin and bank-notes. It has been shewn that coin and notes are valuable only by conventional usage ; and that such value depends upon the existence of the real capital, of which they are no more than the representatives.

This was exemplified by the fact, that the wealth or the poverty of a nation depends, not on the amount of the gold and silver possessed by the people, but upon the buildings, ships, machinery, and commodities in the country ; and that, were we now without these things, and shut out from communion with other countries, we should be no better off than so many starving beggars, even if every individual were possessed of a million of sovereigns ; because there would be no produce to be purchased from each other for the maintenance of life. But, under present arrangements, a man will give up his real capital—his buildings, and machinery, and food—for its worthless representatives, gold and bank-notes ; and he does so only because he is well assured, by his experience of the conventional usages of society, that he can at any time receive for his gold and notes *an amount of real wealth equivalent to their apparent value.* He knows that this money will procure him lodgings, food, and clothing, or any other requisite of life, for twenty or forty years to come, as the amount may be. It matters not whether any of these things be in existence at the time a man receives his money guarantee for them: he knows that there is real capital, somewhere, to the amount of his bond, and that men will toil for and give to him, in exchange for this gold or paper bond, real wealth of every kind to the full amount. It is from these considerations that men buy and sell with money, and give up the real thing for its representative; and upon the same principle, and by the same means, may the working classes purchase from the capitalists all those vast accumulations which the present system of unequal exchanges has enabled them to obtain possession of.

The real capital of the country has been estimated to be worth five thousand millions of pounds sterling; and it has been shewn that the value of the wealth annually produced in the United Kingdom does not fall short of £500,000,000, of which the working classes receive and enjoy less than £200,000,000. If the working classes had only themselves to maintain, at the present rate, and were they to produce annually no greater an amount even than this £500,000,000, they would, in the course of seventeen years, create wealth sufficient to purchase all the present fixed capital of the empire. But it has been shewn that their position, and the enormous burthens which they have to sustain, will ever prevent them from being accumulators to any considerable amount under the present system; and that the subversion of this system, by such means, is an event to be looked for only in the course of centuries, during which the greatest part of the working class must suffer, with unmitigated severity, all the evils entailed upon them by the existing state of things. As it is necessary, however, to the success of any social change, that the real capital of the country should be possessed by the productive classes—as they must acquire such capital by purchase—as they have no means, under present circumstances, of accumulating sufficient wealth to purchase this capital during many generations—it is apparent that the productive classes must still remain the prey and the slaves of their fellows, unless some plan be adopted different to any hitherto made use of by them.

The discovery and adoption of such a plan will be anything but difficult. To accomplish the end desired, let it for a moment be supposed that the desire for a social change is almost universal among the productive classes—that each trade establishes within itself the germs of a future company—that a provisional government of delegates from each is appointed and convened—that paper money, and a coinage of pottery, bearing the two denominations of amount of labour and amount sterling, is created for the purpose of superseding the present medium, and carrying on the future transactions of society—and that a bargain takes place between the producers thus united and the capitalists, and the fixed capital is transferred from the one to the other.

In none of these suppositions—not even in the last—is there anything impossible. It is not indispensable to the success of the movement, that the whole of the capitalists and producers should at once concur in the settlement of the question. The change might be accomplished just so far as there might be capitalists and producers willing to agree in the matter. Assuming, however, that all parties are willing to sell and to buy on the terms proposed—that the capitalists receive their vouchers and give up their property—that the vast amount of unemployed labour and machinery which now exists is set in motion—that new inventions and new appliances are brought to bear in the business of production—that the combined labour and energies of the productive classes are brought into one focus and directed to a common end—the whole of the two thousand millions of debt might be wiped off within twenty years, and the capitalists would be enabled to enjoy this vast sum as they pleased, in the most perfect security, and uninterfered with by the busy world around them.

What are the real difficulties which stand in the way of a transaction such as this? On the one side there is nothing needed but union and industry—on the other, confidence is the sole requisite. The purchase of the real capital of the country, in the manner under consideration, would be as much a legal and proper purchase as any transaction which now takes place between a seller and a buyer.

The magnitude of the contract does not alter its character. If the working classes had gold in their possession wherewith to pay in advance for the things wanted, thousands of capitalists would be willing to make the bargain: and no difficulty would stand in the way of selling the same property to known capitalists, even if they were not possessed of gold, but were simply to give, as security, a promise to pay at some future specified time. If a working man pay gold to a capitalist, or one capitalist pay gold to another, he merely gives a representative of the things which labour *has produced*—if he give a bond to pay at a future time, he merely promises to pay what labour *will produce*. The past, the present, and the future transactions of Capital all depend on Labour for their fulfilment. Such being the case, why should not Labour itself make a purchase? Why should not the bond of *Labour*, to pay at a future time what itself only can produce, be as valuable as the bond of *Capital*, to pay what this very same Labour is to produce? If gold be paid at once to the capitalist for his machinery and buildings, this gold is no more than a voucher that the capitalist shall receive other wealth to the full value of the things obtained from him: if a bond be given, it is equally a voucher that the contract shall be made good. The gold and notes would now be taken by the capitalist for his commodities, simply because the gold and notes form the common circulating medium: and as, in the contemplated change, the notes issued by the productive classes would likewise form the circulating medium, they would in every respect be equally as valuable as the gold. If security be wanted by the capitalist, that the contract shall be abided by, is the security offered by a people of less worth than that offered by an individual? There are innumerable instances of individual breach of faith—the page of history teems with records of governmental treachery—but there cannot be found one solitary instance of the infringement of a contract by a people.

The considerations entered into respecting the wrongs necessarily endured by the working classes under the present system, have shewn us that these wrongs owe their origin to unequal exchanges, and the consequent division of society into employers and employed, or rich and poor; and the first object of every social change is the ultimate subversion of the relations and the inequality existing between these classes. Such being the end in view, it is scarcely to be expected that the capitalists, with their present habits and prejudices, will generally consent even to sell their property for this object. As a class, they will, at the moment, abhor any transaction which tends, however remotely, to take from them their supremacy, to destroy class and caste associations and feel-ings, and to equalize the present distinctions in society. But the inquiry relating to the nature, origin, and trans-mission of wealth has proved that the capitalists, abstract-edly considered, have no rightful title to the land which they now hold, nor to the vast accumulations of capital which they have obtained possession of. The title by which the capitalists hold these things is no more than a conventional privilege—a privilege conferred and sanc-tioned by the common usage of society, without particular limitation as to time. It is likewise a common usage of society, when the property of individuals interferes with the welfare of the body politic—in regard to roads, rail-ways, canals, and other effects—to have such property equitably valued, and, paying its owners the price fixed upon, take the property, independent of their consent. The maintenance of a title to property in perpetuity, without regard to any circumstances which may arise, and independent of any extraneous control, is a thing which even now is never dreamed of. Thus, although the con-ventional privilege by which the capitalists hold possession of their wealth is, in the eye of justice, as sacred as that by which the producers hold the scanty reward of their labour, it is, nevertheless, in the power of society at large to alter at any time its existing arrangements, indepen-dent of the consent of a particular individual or a parti-cular class. But the purchase of the wealth now possessed by the capitalists, in the manner considered, has in it nothing which can tend to interrupt the peace or destroy the happiness of one individual being.

With regard to the union of a number of producers adequate to effect a change in the present system, it is the easiest, as it is the first, step in the movement. Even at the present moment there are no less than two millions of producers united together in societies of various kinds. Almost every working man is or has been a member of a trades' union or trade society; and the number of this class in benefit societies does not, from late returns, fall short of 1,500,000. Those at present united in societies will have dependent upon them eight or nine millions of women and children—the whole mass thus forming no less than one-third of the population. Here is at once mate-rial amply sufficient to accomplish any change, whether social or governmental—material more or less bonded together, and organised, and containing intelligence as well as numbers—material suffering a common wrong from the present state of things, and even now united together for the purpose of destroying or neutralising this wrong. But when the unimprovable nature of the present system is perceived by them—when they become aware of the fix-idity of their doom, and·the utter futility of all mere governmental changes—there can be little doubt that the whole working class will unite as one man to demand a social change; and when they thus demand it, there is no power on earth that can say it shall not take place. This oppressed class alone, if even partially united in one body, and devoting their now divided energies to one purpose, could instantly effect the deliverance of their order and their country—could overturn, by one movement, the whole social fabric, and institute arrangements calculated to produce as much of good and as little of evil as the most sanguine philanthropist can desire.

Such, then, is one mode of accomplishing a social change—such are the means possessed by society for effecting the end desired—such are the results which will follow its con-summation. The object is just, the means are simple, the issue will be satisfactory. The change may for the moment startle some by its novelty, or frighten others who view it through the distorting medium of prejudice; but when the subject has been attentively examined—when the good has been balanced against the evil, the cost against the enjoy-ment—all these feelings of dislike and distrust will insen-sibly disappear, and the whole movement will take the hue and excite only the emotions of an every-day occurrence. In the principles and modes of action considered, neither truth nor justice is outraged—the physical, moral, and intellectual powers of every individual cannot be made worse, but must be made better, by the change—there is no avenue left open through which Despotism, with its

galling fetters and its long train of military and judicial
massacres, can be let in among the people, but every
source of governmental evil will be dried up and destroyed
for ever. There is nothing in the movement which can
lead to social anarchy, or to those innumerable ills which
ever follow in the train of simple governmental revolutions. What, then, has society or individuals to fear?
The productive classes have only to move on with confidence, for Truth is with them—Justice is with them—
all the elements of success are with them !

CHAPTER XII.

CONTRAST BETWEEN THE PRESENT SYSTEM AND THE SYSTEM OF COMMUNITY OF POSSESSIONS.

ALL human ordinances and modes of action are necessarily imperfect, on account of the imperfect knowledge
and the imperfect means of man. As the knowledge of
every man is acquired either through the medium of his
own experience, or the experience of others, he can never,
when attempting to depict a state of things which has not
yet existed, accurately determine how individuals shall
feel and act when placed in these new circumstances and
exposed to these new influences. In looking into the
future, we are compelled to stand upon the past and the
present—to keep experience and facts constantly around
us—to fill up the picture of the unknown by parts
sketched from the known and well-defined. By thus
keeping in view principles, and actions, and incentives
to action, we may make an approximation to, if we cannot
attain, the true result sought for.

The social movement already considered is of this character, and is thus founded ; and therefore, although it
may not be possible to point out every trivial arrangement

which might be adopted by a people acting upon such a system, the principles on which it is founded, and the general outline, will serve as a standard by which to compare and test existing social arrangements. The present generation have no authority over the generations yet to come, and cannot justly institute laws or arrangements which shall be binding upon them. The men of all times are alike free to subvert, to amend, or to institute. There is no such thing as finality; and although, under the existing system, it is the custom of rulers and governments to enact written laws which profess to mark the boundaries within which future opinions and observances shall be confined, yet the time will come when all such records shall be swept away; and there will be sufficient common sense in the world to enable men to decide between right and wrong without appealing to the authority of musty parchments and worm-eaten folios.

The present crisis, whatever it may lead to, is no more than a natural movement attending the course of things— it is but one more of that mighty ocean of events, the billows of which have rolled on from eternity, and will progress in unchecked power for ever. It was fulfilling a predestined move at man's creation—it was advancing as civilization succeeded to the primitive condition of man— it was progressing even when polished Greece and Rome degenerated into semi-barbarism—it was coming on when the French Revolution took place, and Kingcraft and Priestcraft soaked the soil of Europe with blood—and it is at this moment passing before our eyes and bearing us along, destroying and reinstituting, as it always has done and ever will do, political and social institutions of every character and kind. The present is not a merely local movement—it is not confined to country, to colour, or to creed—the universe is the sphere in which it acts, and it operates on all creation. In considering social changes, then, men are in no way restricted in their inquiries by existing arrangements and regulations; nor, in carrying forward the changes contemplated, are they in any way bound by the alleged sacredness of particular institutions, whatever may be their character or their object. All such have been established at various times and for various purposes—they have at like times and for the like purposes been modified and amended—and the men

of the present day have the same right and power to subvert, as the men of former times had to institute and maintain.   All these movements and changes were revolutions ;
and, as every page of history proves, the greater or less
evils which have generally attended such changes, have
been produced by the stupid endeavours of rulers and
governments to convince nations, by the application of the
sabre and the bayonet, that falsehood was truth, that gross
wrong was justice, that slavery was liberty.

Thus free to think and to act—having examined and
tested the various principles and modes of action which are
essential to national prosperity and individual happiness,
and beheld some of the innumerable evils which flow from
their non-observance—we can at once enter into a more
detailed contrast between existing arrangements and the
social system of community of possessions under the modifications already briefly considered ; and likewise examine
a few more of those measures which are contended for by
particular sections of the community, as remedies for
existing evils.

We have supposed that the present distinctions in society, as relating to rich and poor or employers and
employed, are totally subverted—that society is comprised
but of one class, labourers mental and manual, who are
united together in an indefinite number of communities or
joint-stock companies, in which labour is universal and the
remuneration in proportion to the time of labour—that
these communities hold possession of the land and the
productive capital of the nation—that they are likewise
possessed of a circulating bank-note or paper medium,
amounting to two thousand millions of pounds sterling—
and that they mutually and universally produce or distri-
bute wealth, and exchange their labour and their productions on one broad principle of equality.   This vast
confederation of labour has somewhat the character of a
modern joint-stock company, and will bring forth its
results by means of similar appliances.   The more advanced form of community which has been considered, varies
from the movement now under consideration merely in its
arrangements.   Each movement has the same ultimate end
in view ; and each will accomplish the object desired by a
judicious union and direction of vast powers.

In every state of society there must be labour, and

appropriation, and exchanges; and that system which enables men to produce and appropriate the greatest quantity of wealth with the least expenditure of labour, will be the best system, if its transactions be governed by the just principle of equality of exchanges. Under the present arrangements of society we place a clog upon production at the very outset; for we compel vast masses of men to exist in idleness, and thus lose all the advantages which might be derived from their labour. This system, then, does not permit us to create and appropriate the greatest amount of wealth, and therefore it is unprofitable. Neither is the present system united in any way with equality of exchanges, and therefore it is unjust. The power which sets Labour in motion is vested in those who are not labourers—who exist only to consume that which others produce, and to oppress and vilify those beneath them—and who are enabled thus idly to exist and unceasingly to oppress, in consequence of their position in society. The present social system, therefore, is not only unfavourable to production—not only unjust in regard to exchanges—but totally subversive of all equality of rights.

But under arrangements such as those connected with the system of community, which render it imperative on all able-bodied persons to labour, and which assist such labour by every contrivance which ingenuity can invent, there must be vast production. This universal labour, when united with equal exchanges, will adjust all appropriation on the principles of equity. The system of community, moreover, places the national accumulations of capital at the disposal of the nation as a whole—it allows not one man to be in any way subject to the caprice or the mercy of another—and therefore it must ever equally protect all individuals from every kind of tyranny. Thus, whether in respect to production, or distribution, or appropriation—to the saving of labour or the enjoyment of wealth—to the establishment and maintenance of equal rights and equal laws—to all other things necessary to national greatness and individual happiness, the two systems will admit of no comparison.

The general character of the arrangements necessary to carry forward the joint-stock modification of community would be so similar to those at present existing, that particular enumeration will be unnecessary. There would be general and local accumulations or magazines of food and necessaries; this produce would be distributed by means of large markets or bazaars, instead of through the instrumentality of innumerable petty tradesmen; and every necessary and luxury would be procurable in any part of the country for its cost of production in gross, neither depreciated by abundance nor enhanced by the artifices of speculators. The production and transport of all kinds of commodities would be properly regulated and adjusted, and be limited by no restrictions but those which naturally flow from the gratification of all wants. The affairs of society at large would be regulated and controlled by general and local boards of various kinds, the members of which would be elected by the communities. A national bank would create the circulating medium, and issue it to the managers of the various companies in proportion to the number of members in each company, or the character of their occupation. With this money would all individuals and companies purchase commodities and transact their exchanges, on the present principles of trade; and, either by the imposition of a direct tax on persons, or a percentage on commodities, accumulations would be insured sufficient to provide amply for all exigiencies. The money issued would always keep within the limits of the actual effective capital existing; and it would, like blood within the living body, flow equably throughout society at large, and infuse universal health and vigour. The money would always be at hand to pay for the labour—the labour would be ever ready to exert its power for this universal representative—and thus, while the money would insure the labour, the labour itself would insure the creation of the commodities which would be required for the money. There could be no confusion—no gluts—no want of employment—no poverty; but production, and accumulation, and distribution, and consumption, would be naturally adjusted to each other, and would harmoniously work out their common results.

As an example of the working of the system, let it be supposed that there are five companies—composed of about the same number of men, and making use of the same amount of capital—No. 1 being engaged in the production of food, No. 2 producing woollen cloth, No. 3 being employed in the manufacture of cotton, No. 4 acting as a

general home distributor, and No. 5 as a foreign distributor and importer of foreign produce. No. 1 would pay a
certain weekly or yearly sum for rent, wages, and other
purposes ; and the total value of its productions would be
equivalent to the gross amount of money or labour which
had been expended upon them. The value of the commodities produced by No. 2 and No. 3 would be determined
in the same manner ; and the distributors, No. 4 and No.
5, would purchase their commodities from the other companies and from other countries, convey them to the general and local markets, and place upon them a per-centage
equivalent to the extra labour which had been employed
upon their transport and their distribution as a whole.
Upon the same principle, and by the same means, would
production and distribution be regulated throughout society at large—being alternately increased, or decreased,
or turned into new channels, as the exigencies of society
might require. Whatever might be the character of the
labour of these companies, and wherever they might be
situated, every individual member would receive the true
value of his labour in wages, and with these wages he
would purchase commodities of every kind at their true
value—all advantages being equally enjoyed, and neither
individuals nor companies deriving gain from the loss of
others.

As the payment of every member of these companies
will depend upon the condition that he shall labour, it is
certain that work will be performed—if labour be employed upon material, it will shew its results in the shape
of commodities—and thus, for every hour's labour that is
paid for by any community, there will be an equivalent of
some kind for the remuneration given, and this equivalent
will exchange for another equivalent from some other
party. A system like this contains a self-regulating principle such as can never have existence under present
arrangements ; and, while production and distribution and
consumption are linked together, the first and the last are
placed in contact, and a circle is thus formed which enclo-
ses society at large, and places the welfare of every individual at the disposal of himself.

In every social system, the first and most important
arrangements to be considered are those which relate to
the production and distribution of food. The defective

character of these arrangements in the United Kingdom
has long been notorious, and various remedies have been
suggested; but there can be no true remedy in connection
with the present system.   Existing arrangements admit
of individual possession of the soil ; and such possession,
by enabling a particular class to determine upon what
terms and to what extent food shall be produced, place
the bulk of society at the mercy of this class, and expose
them to every species of fraud which avarice can invent.
The exclusive possession of the soil by particular individuals is a social arrangement which has been proved to be
productive of evil under all circumstances ; and, in countries where the land is very limited in extent and unequal
in fertility, individual possession gives rise to institutions
and practices of the grossest vileness and injustice. Under
such circumstances, the proprietor of the land demands
from the cultivator of it, in the shape of rent, a large
share of the produce—he enables the cultivator to give
him such share, by enacting legislative measures which
exclude the corn of countries where the land is abundant
in quantity and inexhaustible in fertility—such exclusion
keeps up the price of home-grown produce to the level of
the rent paid to the proprietor—these exclusive laws are
made by the proprietors in their character of rulers—they
acquire this authority by means of their wealth—they
obtain this wealth as rent, because they claim an exclusive
title to the soil.   Thus does individual possession of the
soil spontaneously generate, one by one, evils which afflict
society at large ; for, by this arrangement, the production
of food is restricted to an extent which dooms thousands to
suffer hunger—governmental despotism is generated—the
labour of a large section of the community is thrown upon
the shoulders of another section—and the landed proprietors of Britain are enabled to suck from the productive
class, in the shape of rent, the greater part of the annual
sum of £100,000,000.

To remedy this state of things, a repeal of the corn laws
is sought for; and it is averred that, if foreign corn be allowed free entrance into the country, home-grown corn must
sink in price to the level of the foreign corn—that, as the
home-corn is reduced in price, the rents of farms must be
reduced—and that, as those rents are brought down, the
vast social burthen imposed upon the working class by the

proprietors will be reduced ; and the greater part of the one hundred millions sterling, now annually lost by them, will be left in the pockets of the producers.

This is a remedy of the same inefficient and fallacious character as those which have been previously examined. It has been again and again proved, that it is the social position of the working class which dooms them to perform a great quantity of labour for a very little reward—that this reward is not measured by the deserts of those who earn it, but by the number of idlers who are to be maintained out of it—and therefore, that any legislative enactment or social regulation which leaves untouched this position and the number of idlers to be supported, must from its nature be useless. That cheap food, in connection with the present system, would produce none of the beneficial effects anticipated, is evident from the condition of the working classes of Europe and of the United States ; for they are compelled by the present arrangements of society, in defiance of cheap food, to maintain a trading and commercial aristocracy in full vigour—competition produces among them its common results—they wander about unemployed in thousands, dependent upon the mercy and the caprice of employers—and the greater part of the wealth which they produce is transferred to other classes by means of unequal exchanges. So long as the present social system exists, it will ever be, with the working man, no more than a choice between two means of losing. What is knocked from the hands of the aristocracy of the land will be instantly snapped up by the aristocracy of the ship, or the mill, or the shop.

The land of the United Kingdom is of various degrees of fertility : some descriptions yield a rich return, and others are not worth cultivating. Under such circumstances, it would be the extreme of stupidity to waste labour in producing corn on the unproductive land, when the corn can be procured abroad at one-half the price. Men work not for the labour's sake, but the wealth's sake ; and all labour must ever be directed so as to procure increased wealth or increased leisure. We must never work two hours to accomplish an object, after a method has been discovered of effecting the same thing in one hour.

The diversity of soils and products which appertain to various countries, enables men to relieve the wants of each other, and thereby tends to draw them closely together in that bond of fellowship which ever exists, more or less, among all beings of one kind. Under the system of society which has heretofore existed—engendering national as well as individual hostility—it may have been advantageous for nations to be independent of each other in regard to food. Had they not been thus, a whole people might have been starved at the caprice of some neighbouring tyrant. This necessity, however, will cease entirely when nations know and act upon the principles of community and equality.

Although all countries are not equally well adapted for the production of food, there are few which do not furnish a material or commodity of some kind for which food can be obtained in exchange. A nation, when considering what it is in want of, should likewise discover what it has to spare, and what is wanted by the people of other countries. Food, apparel, metals, minerals, and timber, are indispensable commodities; and a nation having a superfluity of any one of these things may be certain of obtaining, in exchange for it, any other article of which it may be in want. There is not a people to be found who are not more or less dependent upon the inhabitants of other countries for certain commodities.

The United Kingdom, from its geographical position and its limited extent, is thus naturally dependent upon foreign countries for all its luxuries and the greater part of its necessaries; and, as a compensation and an equivalent, it contains inexhaustible stores of metals and minerals. Science and art, therefore, instead of being directed to devise means by which indispensable commodities may be laboriously and inefficiently produced in Britain, should be applied to discover methods for the cheap and speedy production of equivalents for the things desired. Commodities should never be obtained by creation if they can be more easily acquired through the medium of exchange.

Under the social system of community of possessions the principle of free trade could be carried out to its fullest extent, and its vast benefits be universally enjoyed. Under the present system, however, the interests of individuals and nations are so little understood, and are brought into such perpetual collision and hostility, that a really free trade can exist only in name; and the benefits derivable from an interchange of national commodities will be exclusively enjoyed. The existing state of things incontestibly proves that such is and ever will be the case.

It has long been known that the people of the United Kingdom, although destitute of the raw material of many indispensable commodities, possess every requisite for the manufacture of the raw material into the commodities desired. Attention, therefore, has been directed to manufactures; and machinery, as the first step to manufactures, has been of paramount importance, and efforts have been made to apply it to almost every kind of production. As we have already seen, there is now in the United Kingdom machinery adequate to perform the labour of one hundred millions of men. But, under the present system, this vast power neither lightens the labour nor increases the enjoyments of the working class; for it is in the possession, and works for the exclusive advantage, of other classes. The unrestricted machinery remedy contended for by a section of the economists, therefore, is of the same illusory character as all their other remedies. It does not go to the cause, and it cannot do away with the effect. It has been shewn that the present social system, by unequal exchanges places *the commodities created,* or the capital, on the one side, and *the power which creates,* or the labour, on the other. Labour is the only equivalent which a working man has to give for commodities—every invention which lessens the demand for labour takes away a portion of this equivalent—every increase of machinery displaces particular descriptions of labour, and therefore destroys the equivalent of particular workmen, or brings down its value—and thus, under the present system, and in connection with a comparatively limited amount of machinery, thousands are compelled to starve in Britain amidst glutted warehouses, while the capitalists are traversing the whole earth for customers.

Instead of devising and instituting arrangements which will bring into operation the unemployed labour of the destitute workman, and enable the various sections of the community to produce equivalents and exchange them with each other, the capitalists seek for a free trade to foreign countries, that they may get rid of their commodities among nations who have an equivalent to give for them. An extended market always leads to the increased introduction of machinery and the consequent displacement of human labour—and thus what is called a free trade tends ultimately to lessen the value of the home workman's equivalent, and to take it from him, and to entail upon him years of poverty and suffering, although it for a moment imparts a feverish and unhealthy activity to the body politic. Under the present social system, as it has been shewn, machinery gradually takes the labour, and therefore the food resulting from that labour, out of the hands of the producer, and puts into the pockets of the capitalist all the wealth which is created. Under these circumstances machinery is an evil to the workman; and free trade, as it tends to increase machinery, is likewise an evil; and it is not in the nature of things that the unlimited extension of two great evils should alter their character or detract from their potency.

A free trade and unlimited machinery, although thus fatal to the interest of the producer in connection with the present system, would, under the system of community, confer upon him incalculable benefits. As it has before been said, men want food, clothing, shelter, and leisure for mental improvement and recreation—they want certain *commodities,* and not the *work* which produces them. Under a system of community of possessions, then, where the productive forces of society would be common property, and where all advantages of this kind would be universally and equally enjoyed, a free trade and unrestricted machinery could be productive only of good. The machinery would no longer be an antagonist of the producer—it would no longer work against him, and assist a capitalist to press him into the earth—but it would be a universal friend and assistant; and a free trade, while it carried away all the commodities which he was unable to consume, would bring him, in exchange, the varied treasures of every corner of the earth.

Thus, two of the most important auxiliaries to worldly prosperity which man can make use of—unlimited machinery and an unrestricted trade—must ever, under the present system, not only lose the greater part of their advantages, but be at the same time productive of an immense amount of positive physical suffering and social evil. They are causes of wrong, and, as such, cannot be converted into remedies. With community of possessions,

however, they change at once their present character and
tendencies: they can be known only as great benefits, and
as remedies for a host of evils. Under the present system, and as remedies for existing evils, both free trade and
unlimited machinery are worthless. They do not in the
least change the social position of the working class—they
do not afford this class either increased wealth or increased
leisure—they do not make this class independent of the
control and the exactions of other classes—and therefore
free trade and machinery are not the proper remedies for
the wrongs existing in connection with dependence, and
poverty, and inordinate toil. Such is the vast difference
between the partial and the general possession of mighty
benefits !

Intimately connected with the free trade and unrestricted machinery remedies, and advocated by the same
class, is the remedy of emigration. It has long been seen
that there was more labour in the United Kingdom than
could be employed by the capitalists at any price—it has
for years been felt by the workmen engaged in manufactures, that machinery was slowly but surely taking from
them every thing that can make life desirable, and throwing them upon the world almost destitute of the power of
determining whether they would live or die. As machinery has superseded the labour of the workmen engaged
in particular trades, their wages have come down shilling
by shilling and penny by penny, until at length the most
incessant labour is scarcely adequate to procure the coarsest food. Large masses of men have been placed in this
position ; and a great and gradually increasing portion,
unable to obtain employment on any terms, have been compelled to fall back upon the slender provision which poor
laws yet allow for the relief of the destitute. The remedy
which the capitalist has devised for this state of things,
does not go to the finding of moderate labour and ample
remuneration for the workman—does not go to the equitable division of the wealth which the machinery and the
labour call into existence—does not go in any way to alter
the causes which have induced the present state of things
—but it would expatriate the half-famished workman to
some foreign clime, where his murmurings will be unheard,
his threats unfeared, and his wants unrelieved by the
wretched pittance extorted from capital by means of poor-
rates.

In most of the countries to which emigrants are thus despatched, the land is of a barren description and the climate insalubrious. But, were the soil the best that the sun shines upon, and the air the purest that can be breathed—were such a place all that the heart of man can wish for—it could, under the present social system, be productive of no more happiness or morality than is observable here.   There would be inequality of possessions, inequality of labour, and inequality of exchanges—there would be superiors and inferiors—there would be discord, and envy, and hatred—there would be tyrants and slaves. That such would be the case, is proved by the records of every colony which Britain or any other nation has yet established; and the reasons why it would be so, and be so necessarily, have already been shown.

One of the chief recommendations held out to induce the working classes to emigrate, will be found to contain, if viewed for one moment, a contradiction in itself.   The producers are told that many persons, who emigrate as poor working men, soon become very rich, acquire lands and houses, and *employ many labourers.*   Here is at once a picture of the present system—an acknowledgment that the producers are in all places a doomed class.   In a colony, as well as in a thickly-populated country, one man can become rich only on condition that many shall remain poor—one man is an employer, and obtains labourers by hire, only because the labourers are too destitute to set themselves to work—and such inequality of condition in colonies, and such a division of society into employers and employed, shews at once, if all other proof were wanting, that the remedy of emigration is for the working man no remedy whatever.

Among their other speculations, the political economists profess to have discovered that population has a tendency to increase faster than the means of subsistence—which means, in other words, that more children are born into the world than can be properly provided for—and it is from this inferred, that, even if the system of community were securely established, and every person left at liberty to marry, it would in a short time be impossible to provide a sufficiency of subsistence for all; and therefore an immense amount of poverty would be generated, and men would prey upon each other as they do at present.

Whatever may have been the reasons which led men to this opinion, and however much or little the doctrine may apply to the present system, is now a matter of no moment. The considerations which have been entered into respecting the nature and origin of wealth, shew that, under the system of community, it will be in the power of society to procure subsistence adequate to meet the wants of all the human beings that may be born for thousands of years. Production is now fettered by innumerable chains—it is not dependent on society at large, but awaits the bidding of particular classes—and, instead of breaking the bonds which confine it, and gathering together and uniting its now divided and hostile forces, the economists would restrict population to the capabilities of restricted production.

This remedy is of the same character as those which have been already examined; and it is another blind attempt to relieve a consequence without interfering with its cause. The population want subsistence—the subsistence requires labour and the raw material: the population have the labour within themselves, and the raw material exists on every side of them: but the raw material is left untouched, the labour is unused, production therefore languishes, and the people starve! The very character of the evil suggests at once the proper remedy; and that is, to place the labour and the material in contact, and the pressure of population upon subsistence will be as a story of old times. It is not now the earth which is faulty, nor is the labour faulty, but the social system is faulty which misappropriates the earth and mis-directs the labour. The wrong lies in the system; and a restriction of population, as it will neither set production free, nor give to the producer the fruits of his exertions, will leave the workman just where it finds him—wearied with labour, and "pressing upon the subsistence" allotted to him by Capital.

It is much more easy to find fault with a thing than to amend it. The system of community, as we have already seen, has had its principles decried and its advantages disputed; but wherever it has been placed in juxta-position with the present system, and had applied to it the tests which are known to be good, its excellence has been the more apparent after every trial. The joint-stock modification of community of possessions, dissimilar though it be

to the existing system, is nevertheless of such a character,
that all its arrangements and modes of action may be
tested by the common experience of every man. But, although it has been thus weighed and tried in almost every
conceivable manner that can be of importance, there is no
doubt that ignorance and interest will conjure up imaginary difficulties which it is not possible for reason to cope
with or experience to overthrow.

To enumerate all the evils and wrongs connected with
the present social system would require a recapitulation of
all history ; to bring into view and compare every remedy
which has at times been devised for these evils and wrongs,
would demand a repetition of all the laws which governmental ignorance and priestly intolerance has ever framed ;
and to sum up every advantage likely to accrue from the
system of community of possessions, would require a knowledge of the known and the unknown wants of mankind at
large.

But it is said that the great principle of equality of
rights has been weighed in the balance and found wanting
—that its manifestations have been marked by fire, and
blood, and desolation—that it levels all that is high and
good, and sinks lower still all that was depraved and detestable. The considerations which have been entered
into respecting the nature and operation of the principle
of equality, so far from bringing into view characteristics
such as these, prove most convincingly that such attributes
do not belong to equality of rights, and cannot exist in connection with equality. If devastation and slaughter have
marked the progress of any social movement—and history
tells us that they have hitherto attended every advance of
man—it is not the principle of equality of rights which is
accountable for them. The principle, from its very nature,
can never be productive of such results ; and wherever
liberty is outraged, and life or property sacrificed, it is the
black and bloody spirit of Despotism which is at work, and
not the fair and just principle of equality of rights. A
principle can never violate itself ; and whenever equality of
rights is outraged, and wrong and injustice endured, we
there behold the operation of a principle which is unconnected with and contrary to equality.

When viewed in its just character and proportions —
when stripped of the bugbear garb in which "existing

interests" have clothed it—what is there unseemly in equality of rights? What is there, in a social system founded upon this principle, that honesty would turn from or justice condemn? We have viewed its operation in regard to the production and distribution of wealth, and the establishment of political authority—we have beheld it as influencing and governing every transaction between man and man—and the picture presents a harmonious and well-proportioned whole, comprised of vast powers, immense production, and universal enjoyment.

In the common governmental revolutions which occasionally take place in nations, there is much injustice inflicted, and much blood and wealth sacrificed, by both the oppressors and the oppressed. Such movements rarely rest on principles of any kind ; but society, split up into factions, and led by men having various and dissimilar objects in view, is more at war with itself than with the enemy which is intended to be overthrown. These changes are never more than a succession of tyrannies ; they are generally commenced and carried on for the attainment of exclusive benefits for particular classes ; and they often leave the producers of wealth in a worse condition than they were before the change took place. But the present movement is not of this evanescent and exclusive character —it has no leaders, and no class and caste interests to subserve—it is not to be established by a particular party to-day, and subverted by another party to-morrow. Resting on broad principles, having a clear and well-defined object in view, and embracing society at large, it is of a character altogether distinct from the petty movements which have preceded it ; and, working out its results by means different to any hitherto made use of, the evils which have existed in connection with previous changes have no necessary connection with the present.

The social system of community of possessions is of such a character, that it contains within itself not only all the requisites desired by the economists, but also all the political equality contended for by the politicians ; and it has been proved, from incontrovertible facts, that, under the present system, none of these things can be productive of advantage to the great bulk of society. It has been shewn that existing arrangements tend to create a diversity of interests, and an inequality of condition, and a consequent system of legislation for the exclusive benefit of particular classes ; and under such arrangements it is not possible to devise efficient remedies, nor can just laws and regulations be kept sacred.   But, under the system of community and equality, the insulting tyrant and the trembling slave— the overgorged capitalist and the famishing producer— every social ill and governmental grievance now endured —will be swept away, and the place which has known them will know them no longer.   The present system will then be a memento of the past—a beacon to point out the rocks whereon millions of human barks have been split and stranded—a loathsome shore, covered with broken hearts, and laved by an ocean of human tears !

CHAPTER XIII.

THE ENCOURAGEMENTS AND DISCOURAGEMENTS OF THE POLITICAL ECONOMISTS IN REGARD TO A SOCIAL CHANGE.

As an instrument for effecting the subversion of the present system, and as a preparatory step to the establishment of community of possessions and equality of rights in its most perfect form, there is scarcely to be found one which contains so many facilities as the joint-stock movement, and there is not one against which so few objections can be urged. A movement of this character combines all that is good in the present system with much that is essential to a better system ; and, being founded on well-tried principles, and moving onwards by well-known modes and every-day occurrences, it can sustain no injury from the common war-cry of stupidity and craft, that it is "visionary" and "impracticable." This step simply supposes that the land and real capital of the country are possessed by, and used for, society at large—that this capital is obtained from its present possessors by valuation and purchase—that this purchase is made by the great productive section of the community—that this section is divided into an indefinite number of smaller sections, after the manner of joint-stock companies—that these companies create a circulating medium to the amount of the real capital held by them—that this medium is made use of by the various companies according to the number of their members and the particular branch of trade in which they are engaged—that all these companies, and society at large, buy and sell by means of this medium—that one uniform scale, in regard both to time of labour and amount of wages, exists among

all these companies, and extends to every individual belonging to them—that all articles of produce are valued
according to the labour bestowed upon them—that a common national fund is established, for the construction of
public works, the carrying on of government, the providing
of education for all, and the maintenance of the bereaved
young, the helpless, and the aged ; for the insurance of
property, and for effecting every other object which the
wants and exigencies of society may require.

A social change like this would retain every thing which
is worth preserving in the present system, and instantane-
ously sweep away all those evils which are indissolubly
connected with unequal exchanges, inequality of possessions, and the division of society into classes and castes.
The simplicity and efficiency of arrangements such as these
stand pre-eminent when compared with the gordian com-
plexity of the existing system, in which all interests are
opposed and entangled, in which every productive effort is
comparatively ineffectual in accomplishing the end desired,
and in which there is no power capable of regulating and
adjusting the movements of society as a whole, and directing all efforts, in one harmonious flow, to a well-defined
and proper end. With community of possessions, however, every circumstance relating to the welfare of society
may be effectually controlled ; and the joint-stock modification, by being so constituted as to admit *of individual
property in productions* in connection with a *common property in productive powers*—making every individual dependent on his own exertions, and at the same time allowing him an equal participation in every advantage afforded
by nature and art—is fitted to take society as it is, and to
prepare the way for other and better changes.

In proof that this joint-stock modification of society is
incomparably superior to the existing system, and likewise
as an encouragement to those who will not hear of changes
unless they are supported by the authority of great names,
the leading political economists shall give their testimony,
and express their convictions as to what they deem necessary
for the welfare of society. Some of these extracts were intended as arguments for the maintenance of the present system ; others as attacks upon that system of community of
possessions of which this joint-stock movement is merely a
modification ; and others, again, are acknowledgments that

the present social system needs revision and amendment. That these opinions may not lose their true value on account of popular prejudices against, or prepossessions in favour of, the particular individuals expressing them, all names are omitted ; for those conversant with the works of such writers will at once perceive from whom the extracts are taken. Amongst these arguments, and all others adduced by the same class, there is nothing advanced in support of the existing system which will not afford ten-fold support to the joint-stock system ; and none of the objections urged against the more advanced system of community of possessions will apply to the movement now under consideration.

Respecting, firstly, the necessity of a social change, it is confessed :—

" No thinking man or woman who reflects upon the amount of time, thought, and energy, which would be set free by the pressure of competition and money-getting being removed—time, thought, and energy now spent in wearing out the body, and in partially stimulating and partially wasting the mind—*can be satisfied under the present system.*"

To shew that the remedies now contended for by the politicians have not the power of bettering the condition of the people—that the utmost extent to which such measures can be carried out, even to the overthrow of the monarchy and the institution of a republic, will be all but worthless—the same writer thus alludes to the situation of the people in republican and apparently untaxed America :—

" Are the mechanic and farming classes satisfied? No ; not even they, outwardly blessed as they are beyond any class that society has ever contained. They, too, are aware that life must be meant to be passed far otherwise than in providing the outward means of living. They must be aware that though, by great anxiety, they can obtain some portion of time for occupations which are not money-getting, *there must be something wrong in the system* which compels men to devote almost the whole of their waking hours to procure that which, *under a different combination of labour*, might be obtained at a saving of three-fourths of the time."

" The many who imitate as far as they can the modes of the old world, and cherish to the utmost its feudal prepos-

sessions, will only for a time be able to resist the convictions which the working of republican institutions will
force upon them, that *there is no way of securing perfect
social liberty on democratic principles but by* COMMUNITY
OF PROPERTY."

" When the people become tired of their universal ser-
vitude to worldly anxiety—when they have fully medi-
tated and discussed the fact, that ninety-nine hundredths
of social offences arise directly out of property—that the
largest proportion of human faults bear a relation to selfish
possession—that the most formidable classes of diseases are
caused by over or under toil, and by anxiety of mind—they
will be ready for the inquiry, whether this tremendous incubus be indeed irremovable ; *and whether any difficulties attending its removal can be comparable to the evils it inflicts.*"

This is the evidence of an economist, drawn from a consideration of the condition of a people under a democratic
form of government ; and while it plainly shews that the
wrong is within the system, it affords every encouragement
to replace this system by a better.   Keeping in view the
principles and modes of action connected with the joint-
stock system already considered, we have only, in reviewing the chief points contended for by the economists, to
compare the two systems together.   The superiority of
the system of community of possessions, and the weakness
of the existing system, will be apparent in every instance
It will be seen, likewise, that the principles on which the
joint-stock movement is founded, are those which the
economists allow to be the chief props of the present system, and to be consonant with justice, and practicable, and
efficient in the highest degree.

LABOUR.

" Labour was the first price, the original purchase-
money, that was paid for all things.   It was not by gold or
by silver, but by labour, that all the wealth of the world
was originally purchased."

" Every man in society ought to belong to one class of
producers or the other, or to stimulate production by useful though unproductive labour."

" Till the human race reaches its highest point of attainment, there must be always something more to do ; and *the
more power is set at liberty to do it, the better.*   Till all
the arts and sciences are exhausted, till nature has fur-

nished the last of her resources, and man found the limit
of his means of making use of them, *the greatest possible
supply of human labour is wanted.*"

"While the race at large has still so many wants and
wishes ungratified, it ought to be an easy thing for *any
quantity* of labour which is turned away from one kind of
work, to find employment in another. That it is not easy,
is the fault of the constitution of society, and we should be
far from remedying the evil by repressing the principle
and restricting the power of labour."

The joint-stock movement contains all these requisites
and affords all these facilities in a degree infinitely superior
to the present system.

CAPITAL.

"Capital is that part of the wealth of the country which
is employed in production ; and consists of food, clothing,
tools, raw material, machinery, &c., necessary to give effect
to labour."

"With a population pressing against the means of subsistence, the only remedies are, either a reduction of people, or *a more rapid accumulation of capital.*"

"The wealth of a country may be increased in two
ways : it may be increased *by employing a greater portion
of revenue* in the maintenance of productive labour ; or it
may be increased, without employing any additional quantity of labour, by making *the same quantity more productive.*"

"*There is no amount of capital which may not be employed in a country,* because demand is only limited by
production."

"A new creation of capital is always a benefit to society, by creating a new demand."

"*Large capitals, well managed, produce in a larger
proportion than small.*"

"Where consumers abound in proportion to capital, it is
obvious that the way to bestow most happiness is, not to
take away one man's share to give it to another, *but to do
what is possible toward creating another share,* in such a
way as not to cause more want." For, "Production being
the great end in the employment of labour and capital,
*that application of both which secures the largest produc-
tion is the best.*"

Every thing that is here desired can be at once accomplished under the joint-stock system. Such a system will insure a more *rapid accumulation of capital*—it will *employ a greater portion of revenue* in productive labour—it will, by admitting an unlimited quantity of machinery, make *the labour employed more productive*—it will work by means of *large capitals*—it will *create an additional share* for those who are now destitute, without interfering with the share possessed by others—and it is, throughout, such an application of capital and labour as must secure the *largest amount of production.*

CURRENCY.

" To secure the public against any other variations in the value of the currency than those to which the standard itself is subject, and, at the same time, to carry on the circulation with *a medium the least expensive,* is to attain the most perfect state to which a currency can be brought."

" That commodity is alone invariable which *at all times requires the same sacrifice of toil and labour to procure it.*"

The paper and pottery medium with which business would be transacted under the joint-stock system, combines both the security and the unexpensiveness which is here desired. The foundation of this currency is labour—by whatever denomination called, and however divided, either in pounds and shillings, or in labour notes, it is only intended as a voucher for or a representative of labour—and therefore it is a standard as invariable as any that can be made use of. He who is paid a week's wages in this currency, procures for it precisely what he gave—a given number of hours' labour, or the produce of such labour, from some other person ; and however numerous may be the transactions entered into, or the parties exchanging, one uniform and unalterable measure of justice will be obtained and enjoyed by all.

EXCHANGES.

In the present social system, society is divided into rich and poor, or employers and employed—the last, by their position, being left entirely at the mercy of the first ; and it has been shewn that this division and classification is unfavourable to the creation of wealth, because it allows a vast mass of labour to remain unemployed—that it is destructive of social harmony, becauses it places the interests of men in opposition, and makes the gains of one class to be an accumulation of the losses of another—and that, from thus retarding production, leaving labour unemployed, and bringing men and classes into hostile collision, this division and classification of society is the immediate cause of all the vice, and crime, and misery, which is now committed and endured by civilized man. It has likewise been proved that this state of things is primarily induced, not by inequality of powers in men and classes, but by unequal exchanges. If, therefore, the present social evils are to be remedied, the classification of society and the inequality of condition from which they spring must be subverted ; and this can be accomplished only by the establishment of the just principle of equal exchanges, which will effectually remedy all these evils by removing the causes of them. But the general equality of condition which would be induced by equal exchanges, is, to the capitalist and the economist, the last and the most dreaded of all remedies. They would for ever go on patching and plastering the present system, making another hole by every clumsy attempt to repair one already existing. Their own doctrines, however, if the economists did but see it, are strong arguments in favour of equal exchanges ; and go to shew that equal exchanges is the true and the only remedy :—

" The quantity of commodities produced by *equal quantities of toil and trouble* is not always equal ; but real value depends on *the quantity of labour expended,* and not on the mode in which it is expended, or on the degree of its productiveness."

" Labour is the price that man must pay for all things not spontaneously furnished by nature ; and it is plainly by the *magnitude of the price so paid, and not by the magnitude of the things themselves,* that their real value is to be estimated."

" It is not to any one commodity, or set of commodities, but to some given *quantity of labour,* that we must refer for an unvarying standard of real value."

Here is a recognition of the principle that real value is dependent upon labour ; and the only inference that can be drawn from it is, that all men who perform an equal quantity of labour ought to receive an equal remuneration. Such is one of the main principles of the joint-stock movement, as well as of the more perfect state of society

to which this movement will lead ; and such equal remuneration for equal labour, as it will prevent one man or
class from being supported in idleness and luxury at the
expense of another, must maintain a general equality of
condition.   But, evident as is this conclusion, it appears
not to be perceived, for it has been said :—

   " I so far agree with the co-operators as to believe the
time to be discernible when co-operation, *in a certain sense,*
shall prevail—meaning thereby, when *all interests shall
be harmonised instead of opposed ;* but that this includes
equality of condition, I cannot allow, since varieties of
character seem to me to forbid such equality." The joint-
stock system is no more than " co-operation in a certain
sense," and, from its nature, it must " harmonise all interests," and be subversive of the existing inequality of condition.

   Strange are the inconsistencies into which the economists
fall, in the vain attempt to make the worse appear the better cause.   In regard to the present state of society in its
best form—that of *employing every labourer,* but compelling him at the same time to maintain the capitalist—and
to shew that this state of things is more just than that
which insures employment and support for all—this contradiction is advanced :—

   " This kind of equality [not the equality which would
prevent the poor worker from supporting the rich idler,
but which would merely prevent the rich idler from nominally supporting the poor idler] I am doing all I can to
procure, by doing away with *the protection to some which
imposes burdens on others.*   By the same principle I am
bound to oppose that arbitrary equality which *enriches the
weak with the fruits of the strong man's labour !"*   Herein it is absurdly assumed that the nearest approximation
to equal exchanges which can be arrived at—that which
would give equal remuneration for equal labour—contains
within itself more injustice than those arrangements which
arbitrarily give quadruple remuneration for no labour
whatever!   The supposition refutes itself.   It has been
proved that neither the present system of inequality, nor any
modification of this system, can " do away with the protection to some which imposes burdens on others."   Such
imposition of burdens—such " enriching the weak with
the fruits of the strong man's labour"—is a necessary con-

sequence of unequal exchanges, and is the very aim and
end of the existing system.   It is this great and glaring
injustice which characterises the present in contradistinc-
tion to the desired system.   Similar contradictions and
absurdities are manifest ih every attempt to maintain inequality of condition :—

"Man's nature involves inequality of powers; and this
decree of Providence can never be set aside, or its operation neutralised, by any decree of man that the fruits of
those powers shall be equally divided.   Such a decree involves injustice.   *   *   As long as men are unlike one
another there will be a distinction of ranks, though the
distinction may be maintained by a better principle than
heritage.   Rank and wealth will, I trust, be in time distributed according to natural laws ; but degrees of rank and
wealth there will always be ; and the advocates of a system
of equality would greatly promote their cause by a frank
recognition of this truth.   While all evidence from which
a judgment can be formed is before them, and they come
to a conclusion in direct opposition to the evidence, I cannot, however much I may respect them on some accounts,
think them wise and safe guides of the people.   The necessity of inequality of condition may be established thus :—
*   *   There must be an inequality of physical and mental powers, at all events ; and therefore an inequality in
the produce of individual labour.   No one labours, or ever
will labour, without a view to the fruits ; and those fruits,
however appropriated, are property.   If a giant produces
ten times as much as a dwarf, and each is allowed the same
middle portion of the fruits for his maintenance and enjoyment, is it to be supposed that the giant will trouble himself henceforth to produce more than the dwarf ?"

The whole of these arguments have been again and
again refuted.   It has never been affirmed that there is a
perfect equality of powers in men, or that equal remuneration for equal labour involves perfect justice ; but it has
been shewn that such equality is infinitely more just than
the mode of rewarding labour under the present system.
It has likewise been proved, from "all evidence from which
a judgment can be formed," that inequality of condition, or
the gradation of ranks, is in no way connected with inequality of powers ; but that, on the contrary, this inequality of condition is produced and maintained by unequal

exchanges. " All evidence," also, shews that it is the inferior, and not the superior, powers of society that are
placed in exalted stations and possessed of exclusive privileges; and that the minds which conceive and the bones
and muscles which execute enjoy the least and the worst
portion of their own creations.   There are amongst us
neither giants nor dwarfs in respect to production ; for
civilised society is so constituted—production is so multifarious and varied in its parts—mental and physical powers are generally so oppositely bestowed—that there can be
found no occupation for which some men are not more suitable than others, and in which, however incapacitated for
other pursuits, they will not attain the utmost limits of human perfectibility. If men do not now labour, and never will
labour, without a view to the fruits—if the desire to enjoy
these fruits be the chief spur to industry—it is certain
that men will not labour less cheerfully and industriously
under a social system which gives to each man the *whole
fruits* of his exertions, than they do under the present
system, in which every man toils with the certain conviction
that nearly three-fourths of his just reward will be swallowed up by the exactions of profit and interest, and by
governmental imposts of every kind.   Thus, in whatever
light viewed—whether tested by theory or fact—the present system discloses nothing but weakness and rottenness ;
and is so constitutionally defective and corrupt, its inherent principles of inequality so perpetually operating, that
it always must be, as experience shews it always has been,
destructive of every just governmental institution.   But
there are many other arguments brought against the system of community of possessions, and they all equally
carry their refutation along with them :—

   " When the advocates of a common stock can show that
their system *augments capital and regulates population*
more effectually than the system under which individual
property is held, their pretensions will be regarded with
more favour than they have hitherto enjoyed." It has
been shewn that the joint-stock modification of community
of possessions must, from its principles and its mode of
action, augment and regulate capital to any amount of
population, without having recourse to any of those inefficient expedients which are now devised to restrict popula-
lation to the powers of capital.   Again :—

" Here is an engagement to find employment for all who would not or could not procure it for themselves. Now, as the employment of labour must depend on the *subsistence-fund,* no law on earth can enforce *the employment of more labour than that fund can support.*" The fallacy of this argument in reference to the joint-stock system has already been shewn ; for it will apply only to the present system, with its limited amount of money. There are now implements and machines in abundance to fill the hands of all men—there is no description of wealth which is not wanted—men are supported, in some way, whether they work or not—and they are idle in thousands because the capitalists have not money wherewith to set them to work. If this " subsistence fund" be money, it can be enlarged, as we have seen, to any amount ; if the term have reference to food, clothing, and utensils, glutted markets of every kind shew that there is a stock of these things amply sufficient to supply the whole labouring community of the United Kingdom until their labour has created another stock. The joint-stock movement will do away at once with all these difficulties ; for it will create a representative for this subsistence fund—it will systematically direct the combined energies of the productive classes to the creation of wealth—it will second these efforts by the most powerful machines which ingenuity can invent—and it will thus insure to men the enjoyment of an amount of wealth such as they can now scarcely conceive of. But the present system is of such a character that it will admit of no appliances capable of effecting the ends desired. Although all labour is at all times supported, it cannot always be set in motion ; and even when set in motion, there is no security that it shall continue active—there is no power capable of determining whether " panics" shall or shall not take place, and put a stop to production and doom the labourer to starvation. So long as society is maintained on its present principles, the remedies of the political economists tend only to confuse and bewilder the inquirer ; for they afford no satisfactory solution of the anomalies existing on all sides, and they cannot determine to what extent, or for what time, particular evils shall be endured. That community is the one thing needful, however, is shewn by its adaptation to overcome every difficulty which the economist meets with in the present system :—

" The *power to purchase* (i. e. yield an equivalent for value received) *is the real and the only desideratum.* It is the *incapacity of furnishing equivalents* for the products they wish to obtain, that involves so many in want and wretchedness.   The more, then, that this capacity is increased, and the more the facility of production is increased, the more will the condition of society be improved." What can be a stronger argument, with an economist, for the introduction of the joint-stock movement ?   And, again :—

" Every measure that has any tendency *to add to the power of labour,* or to reduce the cost of the commodities produced by its agency, must add proportionally to our power of obtaining wealth and riches ; while every measure or regulation which has any tendency to waste labour, or to raise the cost of producing commodities, must equally lessen this power.   This, then, is the simple and decisive test by which we are to judge of the expediency of every measure affecting the wealth of the country."   If adding to the quantity of labour have anything to do with adding to its power—if the unlimited application of machinery have anything to do with the increase of this power—then will the joint-stock system bear the test here applied to all measures affecting production.

But it is impossible to notice all the arguments brought forward by the economists in favour of a change, or the contradictions which they fall into when denouncing the system of community.   While one says that "capital is not likely to be cared for when it belongs to everybody, that is, nobody ;" and that "common-stock institutions would soon become as so many workhouses, or pauper barracks ;" another affirms that " the experience of all ages and nations proves that high wages, or *increased facilities for obtaining enjoyment,* are at once the keenest spur, the most powerful stimulus, to unremitting and assiduous exertion."   And, again :—" Give to any people the power of accumulating, and we may depend upon it they will not be disinclined to use it effectively.   *   *   No instance can be produced of any people having ever missed an opportunity to amass."

It has long been a grievance to the capitalist that there should be any poor laws—any arrangements to compel him to refund a small portion of his ill-gotten gains for the support of the unemployed and starving working man. An experiment is now being made to determine whether these laws may be abolished with safety to those accumulations of wealth which rapacity has succeeded in scraping toge-ther. Here is a confession that poor-laws ought not to exist ; and likewise an acknowledgment of the difficulties which lie in the way of settling the matter under the pre-sent system—difficulties which can have no existence in the joint-stock modification :—

" Since indigence occasions misery, and disposes to vice, the welfare of society requires *the greatest possible reduc-tion of the number of the indigent.* * * What, then, must be done to lessen the number of the indigent, now so frightfully increasing ? The subsistence fund *must be employed productively,* and capital and labour be allowed to take their natural course ; *i. e., the pauper system must, by some means or other, be extinguished.* * * None of the remedies have struck at the root of the evil, and none could therefore effect lasting good. The test is just this ; *do they tend to lessen the numbers of the indigent ?"* It is well known how the capitalists would "lessen the numbers of the indigent"—by degradation, and expatriation, and actual starvation. The present system so steels the rich man's heart to every generous emotion—suffers his selfish-ness to reign so blindly paramount—that he unthinkingly strikes a blow at his fellow-man which must ultimately recoil upon himself. The joint-stock system, however, af-fords a natural and a ready means of escape from the evils connected with an indigent and unemployed population ; for it is confessed that—" the only true secret of assisting the poor, is to make them *agents in bettering their own condition,* and to supply them, not with a *temporary stimu-lus,* but with a *permanent energy."*

The admissions of the economists go not only to show that the present social system is radically defective, and that a better may be established, but likewise that the people have a perfect right to institute any changes they may think necessary. In regard to property, one of the great requisites for the subversion of the present system, it is confessed that—" *Property is held by conventional, not natural right ;"* which is a plain admission that the wealth claimed by the capitalist is his only by sufferance, and, therefore, that it must be be given up when this sufferance

wills it.   It is likewise acknowledged that enormous
private property "is the great harbourage of crime and
misery, the adversary of knowledge, the corrupter of
peace, the extinguisher of faith and charity."   It is also
confessed that such undue accumulations are destructive of
equitable governmental institutions : — " Enormous private
wealth is inconsistent with the spirit of republicanism.
Wealth is power ; and *large amounts of power ought not
to rest in the hands of individuals.*"

But the capitalists, half-conscious of the wrong committed by them, and dreading evil in every trivial commotion,
find that the sun of wealth, however brightly it may shine,
affords but little warmth.   Those cannot enjoy present
pleasures who look to the future with doubt or dread ; and
to deter the masses from attempting to obtain changes beneficial to them, whether social or governmental, forebo-
ding Capital thus croaks :—

" Let a nation of twenty millions of people, by any act
of folly, *drive capital away from them,* and famine, pesti-
lence, civil war, midnight murder, rapine, and every other
dreadful calamity would follow the unnatural violation of
the laws of God and man.   The twenty millions would soo
be reduced to one million ; the country would fall back a
thousand years.   We should all be idle, but our idleness
would not feed and clothe us ; we might all desire to labour,
but there would be *no accumulations to give us profitable
labour.*   The friend whom we had driven from us would
never return.   We could not go to the capital ; *the capital
would not come back to us.*"

The preposterous stupidity contained in this idle rant
has been sufficiently exposed already.   It has been shewn
that capital cannot be driven away, nor taken away ; and
that, were every capitalist to depart from the country, and
take away every ounce of gold and silver contained in it,
production might still go forward as effectually, and accumulations of produce be made as securely, as at the present
moment.   The long train of direful calamities here prog-
nosticated would have nothing to do with any such removal
of the capitalists and their money.   As the case stands,
the people *could go to the capital*—they could labour—
they could produce—they could enjoy.   But no such removal of the capitalists, and no other event affecting the peace
or the welfare of society for a single moment, need be anti-

cipated. The change contended for is neither necessarily productive of such a state of things, nor has it, of itself, the most remote connection with anarchy or social disorder. It is simply a trading transaction between man and man—a bargain and sale—in which it is to the interest of both parties that the affair should be equitably and amicably adjusted. Therefore all these doleful forebodings of the evils attendant on certain changes, as they do not apply to the movement contemplated, are of no more weight than the mad outcries of the Chinese, during an eclipse of the moon, to frighten away the dragon they suppose to be devouring her. But there are other prophecies respecting changes :—

" Man must and will be better served as the world grows older ; but it will be *by giving the eternal laws of society fair play*, and not by attempting to subvert them." Such fair play can be given only in a social system of community of possessions. Again :—" An immense majority of every civilised people are verging towards a mutual agreement to give, in order that to each may be given, full measure, pressed down, and shaken together, and running over. Such is the plenty in which God showers his gifts among us ; and such is the manner in which he would have us yield each to the other." Is this a picture of the present state of inequality and injustice in every kind of measure ? —or is it a view of a state of society to come ? And, again :—" Natural affinities are ever acting, even now, in opposition to circumstance. *They will in time direct us to the due control of circumstance.*" It is the one great end of the social change under consideration, to enable men thus to control the circumstances which surround and influence them. Four thousand years have afforded sufficient proof of the incompetency of the present system to give men this power ; and the experience acquired during these successive ages will shortly enable them to construct and establish a system calculated to make man all that he would be. As encouragements, then, to perseverance, the same authorities confess that—

" It is useless to struggle in any way against that progress of society whose tendencies are to make *all of us* more comfortable, more instructed, more virtuous, and therefore more happy. * * It is not for us to point out what may be expected from the collective exertions of society to mitigate or to remove the partial or temporary evils which follow in the train even of improvement. Of one thing we are certain. Society can never interfere to stop the improvement; and if any portion of society, who feel the individual suffering, but cannot see the general good, should interfere, with an unavailing violence, to attempt to check that which must go forward, then the laws of society must step in to protect us all, themselves amongst the number, from the consequences of lawless acts." And this, while it affords encouragement to the fearful and the wavering to go boldly onward in the march of improvement, shews the utter futility of all attempts, by individuals and classes, to retard the common progress of things. And, again :—

"The time will come, trust me, when there will be an end of the system under which we suffer. It cannot always be that the law will snatch the bread from the industrious to give it to the idle, and turn labour from its natural channel, and defraud it of its due reward, and authorise the selfish and dissolute to mock at those who prize independence, and who bind themselves to self-denial that they may practice charity. The time will come, depend upon it, when the nation will effectually take to heart such injustice as this. There is much to undo, much to rectify, before the labours of the poor, in their prime, shall secure to them a serene old age; but the time will come."

Such, then, are the discouragements and the encouragements of the political economists respecting social changes. It is confessed by them that some great change is necessary—that a better state of things must ultimately be established—that the nation may institute any changes which it thinks proper—and they likewise point out the chief principles and modes of action that must be kept in view in any change that may be instituted. Thus every ground of doubt and hesitation is removed, and a broad and solid field of action is presented to the people, even by those adversaries who have heretofore ignorantly doomed them to destruction. The present movement will be but the adding of another link to the long chain of human history; and as one link has never yet been the precise counterpart of another, we need not be surprised or alarmed if the contemplated change be somewhat different from those which have preceded it.

CONCLUSION.

HAVING proceeded step by step through the existing social system, and observed wherein is its strength as well as its weakness—having surveyed one by one its elements of power, and beheld their proper and improper combinations and appliances—having viewed some of the innumerable burdens and evils which this system has for ages imposed upon the productive classes, and examined the various remedies suggested for alleviating or removing the national distresses—it now remains for these oppressed and despised classes to determine whether any and what changes shall take place, and to fix upon a time for action.

Before all things, and above all things, there must be amongst them a wide-spread knowledge of the wrong and the remedy—the means and the end.   Until they obtain this knowledge—until they act in accordance with the dictates of this knowledge, and unite their energies into one mass and direct them to one end—they will continue to be, as they always have been, the tools and the dupes of their fellows.   If there be any among them who are contented with their present position in society and their future prospects—who believe that their Creator made them to be the slaves and the prey of their fellow-men—who are willing, when worn out by years of toil, to lie down on the highway side and die like dogs—if there be any such among working men, they will not ask for a social change; but if there be those who believe that the rights of men are equal—that man can claim no dominion over man—that life was given for another purpose than that of being spent in one unvarying round of incessant toil—then will they demand, and they will have, a change in the present state of things.   If there be any among the middle and upper classes who aspire to no higher gratifications than those which they now enjoy—who find existence, as it is, with no void unfilled, no yearnings unsatisfied, no dark or doubtful futurity—such men will call all social changes visionary ; but if these divisions of society, surrounded as they are by every thing that ingenuity and labour can create, feel that nature requires the exercise of other powers than those of the stomach—that there are within them the germs of faculties and feelings that now find no soil in which to grow—that future security has no firm foundation—they will listen when a change is spoken of ; they will inquire into the nature and intent of life, with all its faculties and capacities, and they will confess that there is much in the present system which needs revision and amendment—that there is much wanting, and much which ought to be altogether annihilated.

In whatever way the existing system of separate individual interests is compared with the system of combined individual interests, the superiority of the latter is apparent in its every modification.   If general physical comfort and security from want be all that is desired, the system of community of possessions and equality of rights is the proper system—if the uniform practice of charity and morality, and the absence of all incentives to ill-will, and the universal spread of social love, have anything to do with a social system, then is the system of community of possessions a desirable system—if the advancement of science and art, the proper cultivation and exercise of the intellectual faculties, and the existence of facilities for carrying into effect every regulation which matured wisdom can devise, be desirable in a social system, then is the system of community of possessions the best of all systems.

Men have hitherto endeavoured to incite each other to good actions merely by inculcating the principles of justice and morality.   Surrounding circumstances—all the motives to good and to bad practices—have never been taken into the account ; and as, under the present constitution of society, the majority of circumstances are unfavourable to the practice of the principles inculcated, these principles are necessarily inefficacious, and all but useless.   Before men can control action, they must control the incentives to action ; for principles are valuable only in proportion as they can be acted upon, and as they apply to the

wants and exigencies of mankind. From the common constitution of things, and their action and re-action upon
each other, it is certain that every man has his price — that
there is a boundary beyond which allurements cannot be resisted—that the absence of an adequate temptation is the
common preserver of all honest men. Principle and profit,
therefore, must ever be on one side; for if they be opposed,
there can be no stability in character, no safe dependence
on virtue, no certainty that morality will always be triumphant. Experience proves the truth of this assertion,
however mortifying it may be to human vanity ; for neither
morality nor religion, of themselves, are capable of impel-
ling men, on all occasions, " to do as they would be done
by." Almost every circumstance by which men are now
surrounded hourly incites them to break through the
observance of this great law, however principle may spur
them on to its fulfilment ; and, therefore, unless these circumstances be controlled and directed so as to conduce to
the end desired, principle will be oftener heard of from the
mouths than perceived in the actions of men. The principles of justice and equality which have been already considered, will thus create and control circumstances favourable to the practice of morality and charity, and thereby
render it more easy for men to do as they would be done
by, than to adopt a contrary course.

Many persons, taking a view of the present condition of
society just as narrow as that of the economists and politicians, ascribe most of the existing evils to the absence of
knowledge amongst the people ; and, to supply this one thing
needful, they would establish a national system of education,
and confer on all men the power of reading and writing.
As present evils, however, depend on the present constitution of society, knowledge alone will not have the power
to remedy them, so long as this constitution is maintained.
Physical comfort is the only base on which popular con-
tentment and social harmony can be reared, and the only
foundation on which knowledge and morality can have a
permanent existence, and work out their proper results.

The cultivation of the intellect—the creation of new
wants and wishes—so far from rendering the body insen-
sible to toil and privation, and the mind callous to degradation and injury, will infinitely increase their susceptibi-
lity to all these impressions, and render insupportable that

which was once an almost unconscious burthen. Know-ledge will conduce to the advancement of virtue and morality only while it is allied to comparative ease of con-dition : if the condition remain stationary, and the know-ledge and the wants go forward, vice and crime will like-wise progress, for they are more dependent on physical dis-comfort than on ignorance.   The discontentment of men arises from the inadequacy of their means to satisfy their wants; and everything which tends to multiply wants without likewise multiplying means—which disturbs the equilibrium naturally existing in connection with a low scale of animal and intellectual existence—will lead to social convulsions, and the subversion of existing systems. Every political demonstration, and every trades' union com-bination, are no more than the workings of intellect to raise the physical to the intellectual man—to increase the means to the wants—to enable conception and execution to keep pace with each other.

While some of the advocates for political changes boldly confess that no beneficial measure can be obtained unless the people have recourse to violence, others maintain that everything may ultimately be acquired by persuasion. The possession of political power will, or will not, benefit the working class.   If it do benefit them, why are the work-ing men of republican America in the situation described ? —and if it be of no use, why should it be contended for in preference to all other things ?   Let it be supposed that universal suffrage and all the other political requisites are obtained—that every member of Parliament is sent by working men, and is himself a working man—suppositions all but impossible to exist conjointly. So long as the House of Lords and the Crown form part of the govern-ment, a parliament of this kind would be fettered in every movement, and every act would be null and void. Let it then be supposed that these two great obstacles to political improvement are removed, and that all governmental power is vested in the productive population—a supposition more improbable than any of the preceding. One of the first acts of a government thus constituted would be to interfere between the employer and the employed.   Laws would be made to increase wages and decrease the hours of labour —machinery would in many cases be put down—the power of refusing employment to obnoxious persons would be taken from the employer—and the commercial regulations of society would be subject to perpetual variations to meet the emergencies of particular classes of producers. All these would be social changes—they would affect the relative position of the classes now constituting society, without remedying the evils dependent on this division—and production would be carried on by complicated and ever-changing arrangements—alternately depressing one class and exalting another, and making society a hot-bed for tyranny and hatred.

All the changes contended for by the politicians or the trades' unionists, must, to be effective, interfere with the existing arrangements of society, and thus would be, in reality, social changes. It is as plainly perceived by the capitalists that such would be the case, as it is perceived by them that the workman is discontented with his lot. The wants and wishes of the producers are seen in all their actions, and shine forth in all their movements. Such being the case—seeing nothing before him but the seizure of his property and the subversion of his authority if the working men obtain political power—is it to be supposed that the capitalist will put a weapon into the hands of his natural enemy—that he will, by giving political power to his serf, run the risk of losing his own station and accumulations without any equivalent? Little is known of human nature by those who suppose that the capitalists or their government will commit such a suicidal act unless compelled by the physical force of their adversaries. The intellectual powers of the workman are held in so much contempt—he and his capacities are so thoroughly derided and despised by the other classes of society—that everything calculated to benefit him in the remotest degree, or to take anything from the dominion of the capitalist, will be withheld until the last moment that it can be retained with safety to the powers that be. Thus, as political power, of itself, would be so unwieldy a weapon in the hands of the working man—as every probability is against the acquisition of such power by any means short of physical force—it cannot for a moment be weighed against the safer and more equitable mode of going at once into that state of community which must ultimately be the end of all these other changes; and this can be done by means of purchase, without the application of force or the accompaniment of civil commotion.

In regarding any and every remedy which real or pretended friends may offer to them, the working class should take a broad and comprehensive view of their present position as a whole—the amount of their toil, their dependence on and subjection to other classes, the inadequacy of their remuneration, and their probable condition in old age—and test all these remedies by the influence which they are likely to exert on this position. When the producer is told to seek for the acquisition of political power—to contend for this or that particular governmental measure—he should inquire of all who would direct him :—" Will this change lighten my toil, increase my enjoyments, add to my independence, insure me work and remuneration until age, and then support me comfortably until death ?" It is to acquire all this that men ask for changes, and it is for the opposite state of things that they want a remedy. Every remedy, therefore, which shrinks from the application of the test of equality of rights—every remedy which professes merely to modify the position of the working class *as a working class*—every remedy which does not go at once to first principles, and tend to the removal of the causes of existing wrongs and evils, should be scouted as insulting alike to reason and to justice.

In the conflict which is now going forward between Might and Right, and while men are contending as to whether force or reason shall be the weapon made use of, the experience which former times afford of the operation of these two powers must not be neglected. Such considerations, however, do not affect the establishment of the system of community of possessions ; for this depends not upon force, nor upon impressing the government with a conviction of its necessity, but upon the acquisition of a sufficient fund to purchase the existing accumulations either at once, or by instalments paid after obtaining possession, on the principles already explained.

There have always been two ways of accomplishing merely governmental changes—one, by persuasion, and the other by compulsion. For popular revolutions to be effectual, conviction must always precede force ; for force may establish, but it cannot always preserve. When a people have no knowledge of human rights, they may be persuaded to submit to despotism, or they may be forced to submit : when they possess this knowledge in a limited or imperfect degree, it is possible that a people may overthrow their government; but, if they thus succeed, it is almost certain that they will lose all the benefits of their conquest. When, however, the knowledge of principles is widely spread, and the desire for change is as universal as the knowledge, then is a nation unconquerable, and no power can long exist in opposition and hostility to the popular power.

But, omnipotent as is the might of the oppressed when it thus meets hand to hand the might of the oppressor, there is not one instance on record which shews that the people of a nation have ever yet obtained the fruits of the victory which force had won for them. They have never yet done more than build up a fresh tyranny with the frag_ments of that which they had pulled down ; and so long as they leave unregarded and unregulated that prin_ciple of unequal exchanges and that inequality of condition from which every tyranny springs, all their appeals to phy_sical force, and all their subversions of despotic govern_ments for the time being, will in no way advance the pro_gress of true liberty. The establishment of the proper remedy does not depend upon the subversion of a govern_ment, but upon the destruction of the existing social sys_tem ; and therefore reason, and not force—conviction, and not compulsion—purchase, and not plunder—a systematic application of combined forces, and not an undisciplined and chaotic movement—are the proper instruments to be employed.

The correctness or incorrectness of the estimates which have been given of the burthens imposed upon the pro_ductive classes by the present arrangements of society, is of no importance. These estimates serve as elucidations of the existing system ; and a momentary glance at the pre_sent state of society, and the income of various divisions, will shew at once that the losses of the producers have not been over-rated. Although some of these burthens may be lightened, and many existing social evils may be modi_fied, by particular governmental measures, yet such partial alleviation affords no ground for the maintenance of the present system. All existing wrongs are wrongs on prin_ciple—wrongs on reason, and justice, and equal rights — and must therefore be subverted on principle.

As the knowledge of the character and tendencies of the present system becomes generally diffused—as the produc_

tive classes are brought to direct their attention to a
social instead of a governmental change—as they begin to
unite their scattered forces, and to adopt means for carrying their objects into execution—as all these preparatory
movements are going forward, many false prophets and interested advisers will rise up and endeavour to mislead and
delude the people. When, likewise, the nature and magnitude of the end to be attained is considered—when it is
viewed in connection with the present composition of
society, and the ruthless and sanguinary character of the
governments which arise from society thus constituted—
there can be no doubt that senatorial harangues and pulpit
fulminations will follow each other in quick succession
against all innovators of existing usages. The page of
history, fraught with many a brutal and bloody record of
governmental despotism, gives warning, also, that, when
vituperation shall have exhausted all its materials in con-
demnation of a social change, the weightier arguments of
the cannon and the musket will not be far off. Considerations of this character, however, do not concern the
inquirer after truth, nor do they in any way invalidate the
principles which he may bring to view. Individuals have
not the power to decide in what manner particular changes
shall be accomplished. Placing their trust in principles,
they calmly await the issue of events. There are manifestations on all sides which tell men, in accents not to be
misunderstood, that the elements of mighty changes are
at work; and, whatever may be the immediate prospect,
there are to be seen harbingers of brighter and better
times. The light of Mind is beaming through the gloomy
boundaries of the Age of Might, and ushering in the Age
of Right!

THE END.